·8207 Eng,

ENGLISH IN PRACTICE

LITERATURE AT 'A' LEVEL

Edited by
ROGER KNIGHT

SCOTTISH ACADEMIC PRESS
EDINBURGH
1989

Published by
Scottish Academic Press Ltd.
33 Montgomery Street
Edinburgh EH7 5JX

First published 1989
ISBN 0 7073 0580 2

British Library Cataloguing in Publication Data
English in practice: literature at "A" level.
1. England. Secondary schools. Curriculum subjects:
English literature. teaching
I. Knight, Roger
820'.7'1242
ISBN 0-7073-0580-2

Printed in Great Britain by Page Bros (Norwich) Ltd.

Contents

Contributing Authors

Ian Brinton	is Head of English at Sevenoaks School
Paul Dean	is Head of English at Portsmouth Grammar School
Gerald Gibbs	is Head of English at Woodlands School, Derby
John Haddon	is Head of English at the Hatton School, Derbyshire
Sue Hills	taught English until recently at Burnt Mill School, Harlow
David Huband	is Head of English at Burnt Mill School, Harlow
Roger Knight	is Senior Lecturer in Education at Leicester University and editor of *The Use of English*
Helen Lewis	is English Adviser with the Gwynedd Education Department
Bryan Robson	is Head of English at St. Paul's School, London
Stafford Sherlock	is Gwent's Staff Development Officer for English
Andrew Spicer	is Head of the English section at South Bristol College
Gillian Spraggs	teaches English at the Gateway Sixth Form College, Leicester
David Walton	is Head of English at Homelands School, Derby
Michael Williams	is Head of English at Gedling School, Nottinghamshire
David Williamson	taught English until recently at King Edward VI Grammar School for Girls, Handsworth, Birmingham

Prefatory Note

In their earliest form the majority of the contributions to this book appeared as articles in *The Use of English*. Those dealing with specific authors and texts were in the continuing series 'Teaching the 'A' level text'. In bringing them before a wider audience of English teachers we hope that they may both serve as a demonstration of good practice and provoke debate about the principles that should inform the teaching and the examining of English at 'A' level.

INTRODUCTION

ROGER KNIGHT

There are still critics of formidable reputation who are prepared to speak of 'the classics' and to come up with good traditional reasons why we should read them. 'The classics', said the Italian novelist and critic Italo Calvino, are the books of which we usually hear people say 'I am re-reading' and never 'I am reading'.[1] One question that Calvino does not consider is how a classic work comes about. The omission isn't lazy or careless. It is, almost certainly, because as an artist and critic he is sympathetic to a tradition which, until very recently, was active in the thinking of anyone who spoke on the subject of an established literature. Speaking of 'how a classic inveterately grows', an earlier critic-artist—Henry James— said that its significance 'comes by a process slow and small'. It is a matter of 'perceptive private readers'. While 'plenty of other much more remarkable books come and go', James shrewdly observes, those readers 'accumulate and count. They count by their quality and continuity of attention'. ('The Art of Fiction').[2] Those books that 'come and go' (James's example is George Sand's 'romances') are 'excellent reading for once, but they lack that quality which makes things classical—makes them impose themselves'.

This attribution of an apparently objective power to great works of art is far from idiosyncratic. Coleridge says of the 'single perfect word' in Shakespeare that it gives us that feeling of reality which 'heats and burns and makes itself felt. If we do not grasp it, it seems to grasp us'. Seamus Heaney speaks of 'the mountain (Ben Bulben) which W. B. Yeats was to impose upon the imagination of the modern world'.[3] The imaginative power belongs to the world of the classic writer. 'What such worlds have in common', says John Coulson, 'is their power to place us under their judgements: they are not where we claim but where we are claimed'.[4]

To document the tradition represented in these quotations is to focus a vocabulary and a set of assumptions that have in recent years come under severe attack. Who are those 'perceptive readers'; on what grounds are we to trust the 'process' by which they come to 'count'; at what cost do such readers 'impose' the status of classic on some works rather than others? Aren't Coleridge and Heaney ingenuous in neglecting the social and institutional factors that grant Shakespeare and Yeats the right to 'continuity of attention' in the first place? Isn't it naive to assume an objective power in their writing, a power apparently exercising itself unaffected by

1

time and place? If we are 'claimed' or 'imposed upon' by a writer's imagination, what of individual judgement, what of our creative contribution as readers? Surely we are now wiser than Matthew Arnold was when he approvingly quoted Sainte Beuve's appreciation of the French Academy as 'creating a form of intellectual culture *which shall impose itself on all around*'?[5] Doesn't that traditional vocabulary invite the stultification of thought and practice that can make the study of literature a matter of genuflection before 'inert texts'. Well, it certainly *can*. There is no doubt that some 'A' level literature practice reflects the kind of ossification we intend when we speak of received opinions and standard views. However, before turning to such stultifications and what in practice may be done about them, it is as well to concentrate on the strengths of that unfashionable vocabulary and what it means to teachers of literature. For it is no exaggeration to say that unless it is essentially true, we don't have a subject for study.

Quiller-Couch, early in the present century, wrote that 'the first obligation we owe to any classic, and to those whom we teach is to treat it *absolutely*: not for any secondary or derivative purpose . . . in short we should trust any given masterpiece for its operation on ourselves and on others'. What is important is that a teacher should 'get the attraction to seize upon the pupil. He and the author between them will do the rest: our function is to communicate and trust'. The essays here on *As You Like It* and on *Hopkins* demonstrate that such trust does not mean uncritical self-efface-ment. However, to many modern ears Quiller-Couch's words will seem positively craven in their willingness to accept such entities as 'given masterpieces' (given by whom? it will be asked). Not to all, however. The contemporary American novelist John Barth speaks in tones very different from Quiller-Couch's but his view both of literature and of the teacher's function is similar: 'A beginner . . . needs to be taught that literature is there; here are some examples of it, and here's how the great writers do it'.[7]

A deceptively simple formulation; for some, indeed, scandal-ously simple. What 'teaching that literature is there' can mean is illustrated in Roger Shattuck's remarkable essay 'How to Rescue Literature'. Robustly sceptical about the contribution of con-temporary critical theorists to the teaching of literature, Shattuck argues for the restoration of 'oral interpretation' as a fundamental practice: 'At least for literary criticism as it is practised in the classroom and lecture hall, the acid test is not the intellectual brilliance of the teacher's argument but the demonstrability of the interpretation when he (or someone else) reads aloud a sizeable passage'. Shattuck presents us with a cameo of Ancient and Mod-ern. There is the elderly professor (in an American university) whose seminars on Cervantes consist largely of his reading the text aloud with 'a running commentary on the language, historical background and cross-references in the novel'. Little given to explication and interpretation he is nonetheless a teacher of literature in a tradition Shattuck evokes in describing his 'expressive and very clear voice. His histrionic gestures and shifts in emphasis played constantly between the comic and the passionate'. There is no doubt of his ability to 'get the attraction to seize upon' his students. However 'some faculty members considered Professor M's teaching the scandal of the Spanish department', particularly when measured against 'intense young' Professor N, building a reputation on 'articles combining communications theory and speech-act theory in an analysis of comic strips', and strongly fancied for promotion.

Roger Shattuck's irony lies lightly over the contrast between Professor M and Professor N but the drift of his sympathy is clear. Professor N, Shattuck surmises, would probably feel 'a certain malaise about a Great Tradition and about attempting any form of appreciation, a word now consigned to music departments'. He would thus, one imagines, be sympathetic to that mode of materialist analysis which sees the development of English studies in the universities of Great Britain as a successful conspiracy of bourgeois culture:[9] a conspiracy institutionalised first in their English departments and subsequently in the educational system as a whole. At the extreme we find people—teachers indeed—who look forward to the day when 'words like "culture", "politics", even "literature" with their ingrained accents of possession, separation and exclusion no longer have any meaning for us'.[10] By which time of course, the subject matter of the present book will be obsolete.

Such statements are still, for the most part, seen for what they are: extreme. However, the penetration of such materialist thinking is clear if we consider the vocabulary it proscribes or subverts. 'Cultivation' and 'sensibility', according to a recent writer addressing teachers, are words 'made virtually obsolete by their clear class overtones', a symptom of a 'bourgeois hegemony'.[11] Similarly, another writer thinks it 'very important to let students (at 'A' level) see that literary criticism is not a mystique, or a gift of sensibility, but is dependent on shared concepts of the conventions and codes by which meanings are constructed';[12] thus ignoring the fact that without educated sensibility you cannot judge the quality of what is being expressed through those conventions and codes. (You cannot see, as Eliot sees in Middleton's *The Changeling*, that 'underneath the convention there is the stratum of truth permanent in human nature'). In such a reckoning 'quality', like James's 'process slow and small', ceases to be of much interest. We obviously cannot speak of a 'literary culture'—indeed we can hardly speak of English literature at all—if 'texts, readers and meaning are all subject to the licensing authority of the university'.[13] If we convince ourselves that that is all there is to be said on the subject, then it is easy to dismiss those who select the books for study as 'self-appointed custodians of English literature',[14] to lump them amongst those assumed insensitive, for instance, to the fact that Shakespeare's plays 'carry an elitist tag which excludes them from the legitimate business of a world defined by *Brookside* and *East Enders*!. The same writer says that 'in rejecting Shakespeare . . . drama teachers have responded like many of their colleagues in English departments to an increasing impatience among their pupils with respect to the iconography of bourgeois culture'.[15]

Of course, if the centre of interest for you is not the actuality, the distinctive *quality* of a work of art but its supposed location within a class-derived iconography, you are not going to be much interested in 'getting the attraction' of Shakespeare to 'seize upon' young minds. It is going to be 'notions of Shakespeare as cultural product that matter'. The worst betrayal—not of the literature but of the young—is in the stupefying assumption that 'the world defined by *Brookside* and *East Enders*' is axiomatically of greater significance and value to them. We are, thankfully, still a long way from the decadence of those American universities where—as Rene Wellek reported in *The Attack on Literature*—*Tarzan*, *The Wizard of Oz*, Mickey Spillane's *The Big Kill* and *The Story of O* are included in Literature courses.[16] As Wellek says, 'We cannot get around the question of quality, which is the central question of criticism'. We can, however, *seem* to get around it: by ignoring it, like the NATE writer who, wanting 'a radical change in the way texts are selected' and wishing to 'start from the standpoint that reading is fun' offers this as a principal criterion: 'to validate work by women both for its own sake and for the light it sheds on cultural history'.[17]

Mickey Spillane undoubtedly sheds light on cultural history too. But then, what doesn't? The criterion is not one of 'quality'. It is inimical to quality, to the notion of an inherited culture sanctioned by 'continuity of attention' amongst 'perceptive, private readers' (the only kind of 'validation' that matters). James's stress on the private is akin to Leavis's insistence that judgement is nothing unless it is personal. Which does not mean merely personal: to be a perceptive reader is to be an experienced reader, one whose judgements insensibly form themselves through a wealth of previous encounters with works of literature but are also modified and checked by the judgements of those we recognise as qualified to make them. The current emphasis upon 'the reading process', which might in its turn seem to echo the stress on the 'private' and the 'personal', is indeed in many ways healthy (see Helen Butler's essay here). However, it can also run to a damaging solipsism: 'In most 'A' level English examinations, students are expected to make value judgements about the respective merits of works of literature without a corresponding attention to the reading process that produces these values'.[18] But if those values are 'produced' by the reading process alone (the writer wishes 'to give the reader priority and not the text') we have no criterion for choosing the books to be read in the first place. We have rejected the contribution of culture, of that 'continuity of attention' out of which it had been thought classic works emerged. In practice it can mean that in the absence of any strong belief in the traditional mode of thinking about classic texts, new and tendentious criteria are invoked. If the priority is that students should be 'making meaning for themselves', if the reader is to be given priority over the text, then it is a short step to demanding that what is studied should reflect the present political or ideological interest of the student or teacher. 'The struggle to win the vote' may have 'given rise to an enormous and varied literary output'[19] but that is neither here nor there if our overriding criterion is, as it should be, that the work studied should be outstanding of its kind. Dale Spender's *Mothers of the Novel* (Pandora 1986) shows us what happens when a determination to reclaim forgotten women writers and establish their place within a revised canon is unrestrained by considerations of quality. Is *Bread and Roses*, the Virago anthology of women's poetry from World War One, an 'A' level text on grounds of quality alone?

Are these actually fairly esoteric controversies? To judge from the texts set by the examination boards at 'A' level it might seem so. However, it is clear that we are moving into a period where, with the GCSE as a precedent and an example, pressure will grow for change at 'A' level too. Changes in modes of assessment (and thus of teaching) are certainly overdue, for reasons set out below. However, there are aspects of the GCSE which we should look to as a warning rather than as an example. The SEC's *Guide for Teachers of English* (1986) insists that there must be 'cultural diversity in the literary texts studied' and that 'the "traditional" canon of English literature should be widened'. That might have been an invitation to seek out the best writing in English from all parts of the world. That is how the best teachers will interpret it. However, the SEC's conception of cultural diversity is glossed in a manner that robs the traditional terms of all their traditional force: 'In exercising your freedom to select texts you will need to make sure, for instance, that the range of texts offered relates equally to the interests and experiences of girls and boys, and meets the requirements for ethnic and political balance'.[20] There, again, is the notion of literature as 'cultural product', a warrant for James Gribble's view that 'it is widely assumed by English teachers that literature is just a semi-fictional way of analysing moral and social problems'.[21] George Eliot said that art that 'lapses anywhere from the picture to the diagram . . . becomes the most offensive of all teaching'.[22] To think that considerations of political balance are relevant to the discussion of literature is to see it as a collection of diagrams rather than as images of life. 'At least one spirit of the age', says Seamus Heaney, 'will probably be discernible in a poet's work (but) he should not turn his brain into a butterfly net in pursuit of it'.[23]

If we are to see the growth of 'alternative' 'A' level syllabuses in the coming years it is vital that it should be on the basis of a much more sophisticated notion of literature than the SEC offers for GCSE. At present the 'A' level Common Core agreement[24] binding the boards stipulates only that the minimum selection of six texts should include a Shakespeare play and one pre-twentieth century work. One board, Cambridge, would be prepared to jettison the second part of that stipulation. If, with the spread of alternative syllabuses, and greater freedom amongst teachers to choose texts for study, the selection is governed by criteria as questionable as those reviewed above, we shall face a dilution that could effectively be the death of the subject.

For instance, if we start from the assumption that reading should be 'fun' and that 'enjoyment and pleasure are the first criterion for wanting to study literature', we can quickly convince ourselves that the freedom available under the Common Core agreement should be exercised to exclude works that declare their character only after much patient and sustained attention, works where the only 'pleasure' worth having has to be worked for in a way never demanded by activities that are 'fun'. We can easily be persuaded that it is only works of contemporary literature that are likely to meet our criteria. Pope, Johnson, Milton, Jane Austen, Wordsworth, Yeats – *'fun'*? HMI seem close to thinking they ought to be. 'Much time', they say, 'is lost in the teaching of 'A' level literature by the assumption that the language of literature itself is difficult, mysterious and obscure'.[25] Those who make that assumption are in good company. Kathleen Raine, speaking of Yeats, talks of 'the magic of words in their power not merely to describe but to create their own universe'. Yeats's writings, she says, first captured her imagination because they 'realised the invisible country of the soul'.[26] Seamus Heaney confesses to 'listening' for poems which 'come sometimes like bodies out of a bog, almost complete, seeming to have been laid down a long time ago, surfacing with a touch of mystery'.[27] And the mystery belongs not only to the origins of art but to the pleasure and benefits it brings. James describes it as an 'eternal mystery' that we receive such satisfaction from looking into 'another world, another consciousness'.

Since HMI so lightly and fashionably discount that traditional idiom, that consistency of opinion and feeling amongst the practitioners, how would they defend the centrality of the practical criticism paper at 'A' level? How do the Examination Boards defend it (the Working Party considered making it part of the common core since for six of the nine boards it is already compulsory)? For the practical criticism paper, with its roots in the Cambridge School of English of the twenties and thirties, owes its presence to an acceptance of that traditional idiom. It assumes that 'literary culture' is a reality, that the powers of critical judgement it tests have been developed through rigorously critical reading of the very demanding works of literature that constitute such a culture. Above all, it demands breadth of reading. And breadth is what the Common Core agreement positively discourages.

The practical criticism paper ('unseen critical appreciation') has always been problematic and should be more controversial than it in fact is. That it throws so many candidates into depression and panic and back upon desperate remedies of the kind perennially chronicled in examiners' reports is not surprising if we reflect that the ability to be intelligent about sophisticated work never before encountered is a rare enough accomplishment amongst highly educated adults. Amongst adolescents who cannot be expected to have secured the necessary breadth of reading and engaged in mature reflection upon it the exercise is bound to expose their weaknesses and lead to false conclusions about their real abilities. Given that passages for 'unseen appreciation' may be taken from any period, the disasters invited by the practice are likely to be even more numerous amongst those whose set texts may have included no more than two works written before the present century. (Unsurprisingly the Cambridge board reports its optional critical appreciation paper is not a popular choice: it would, one imagines, be even less welcome to candidates if Cambridge's proposal that the selection of books might be limited to the twentieth century had been accepted.)

The contradictions to be found in the Examining Boards' prescriptions are not of course in themselves a reason for arguing for the abolition of the practical criticism paper. The most able (particularly if their study of set texts is supplemented by the kind of broad and guided reading described here by David Williamson) will continue to do themselves justice. However, that it should be a compulsory paper 'accounting for between 20%–33% of the total marks' is indefensible. The principal reasons are set out in 'Practical Criticism Examined', within. There are others: the present emphasis upon forms of writing anterior to the fully articulate critical essay is not one we can expect to be displaced. If the notions of a canon and a classic text have come under a challenge that ignores the witness of the practitioners, the same cannot be said about the reaction of English teachers to our increasing knowledge of the processes by which good and great writers alike commonly arrive at their eventual goal. 'First drafts', says Bernard Malamud, 'are for learning what your novel or story is about'. Stephen Spender reckons to work through no fewer than a hundred re-writings before putting his name to a poem. Marquez writes a paragraph of four or five lines in as many hours – 'which I usually tear up the next day'.[28] Anthony Thwaite reports Larkin's poem 'The Whitsun Weddings' as going through thirty pages of drafts over many months – a matter of 'testing, filtering, rejecting, and modulating'.[29] What, on the other hand, we ask of examination candidates is that they skip those preliminary, ruminative, tentative stages of writing and move instantly into the top gear that produces the supposedly definitive expression of their ideas and response. It is no wonder that for all the acknowledged good work produced despite conditions so unfavourable, examiners' reports strike a perennially melancholy note. The only remarkable aspect of this continuous lament is that examiners never admit their own responsibility for the conditions that provoke it. Reports on candidates' performance in the critical appreciation paper are only the most conspicuous of the examples that can be quoted. Year after year we can with absolute certainty expect very slight variations on the dreary theme: the 'mechanical listing of technical features and figures of speech' (Oxford 1984); 'the Mrs. Beeton approach which lists by quantity the various stylistic ingredients' (London 1987); the 'cataloguing of alliteration, assonance, metre and rhyme scheme (will act) as a defence against having to come into contact with the meaning of the poem in question' (Cambridge 1987). A.E.B.'s vocabulary over the years is as predictable as the deficiencies it records: candidates 'worked grimly through their prepared shopping list . . . having armed themselves with a check-list of technicalities' (1984); they have 'a tendency to go through a check-list of stylistic features (1985); they 'continue to do little more than produce a list of devices' (1986). Inevitably the 1987 report simply records the persistence of 'the common habit of making long lists of images and of unusual words—an absolutely valueless exercise'.

It is a ritual. We are looking at a serious paralysis of understanding—not amongst the candidates but amongst the examiners.

It is a paralysis that bears the unmistakable mark of failure to face up to the obvious. Into the Cambridge examiners' comments (1987) has come a sharper note of alarm that says much about the problems we face: 'Examiners were deeply perturbed by the dramatic increase in the use of study notes as a substitute for first-hand contact with Shakespeare's texts'. Oxford's (1984) ingenuous complaint that candidates don't 'think freshly in the examination room in response to unfamiliar questions' but 'take refuge in reproducing previously prepared work'; the suspicion of the Cambridge examiners (1987) that insecurity tempts candidates into a half-hearted regurgitation of a 'safe' line; the same board's observation of *Hamlet* 'providing the most spectacular example of students clinging at all costs to the received critical life-line of their study notes'— these are as familiar as the expressions of regret that candidates resort to 'all-too-frequent ritual character-sketching', again probably 'parrotted from the study notes' (London 1987). As familiar, too, as the examiners' failure or unwillingness to recognise that the ever proliferating life-lines spun out by competing publishers are positively invited by the system that the examiners administer. Whilst the stand-and-deliver convention of the end-of-course examination survives, there is no chance of the abuses so predictably catalogued by the examiners diminishing. A convention that must tax the most gifted inevitably drives huge numbers of candidates into the willing arms of those who wait in the market-place. Bill Greenwell's NATE booklet (1988)[30] makes it clear that the growth of alternative 'A' level syllabuses does not necessarily imply a widespread attempt to tackle these problems ('many are mutton dressed up as more palatable lamb'). However there is no doubt that those syllabuses which place a strong emphasis upon assessment through coursework and extended essays (see Andrew Spicer's contribution here) are making a much more intelligent response to the habits of mind of which the 'A' level examiners complain than the perennial bouts of handwringing and despairing exhortation to be found in the reports of the examiners themselves.

It is a commonplace that examinations should encourage and support rather than impede good teaching. They should, in short, be worthy of the quality of English teaching described in the present book. These essays do, I hope, amount to an answer to the question: where do good English teachers stand in relation to some of the issues broached above? These teachers are alert to fresh thinking, criticism and innovation in the area of literature teaching. And they are united in their attachment to and belief in its importance – which is not to say that they set up as 'custodians', genuflecting and compelling others to genuflect before 'inert texts'. Whilst sharing the healthy conviction that all questions of judgement and response are in some degree permanently open, they are at the same time aware that their authority and responsibility as teachers draw strength from the literary culture of which the particular text is a small part. There are examples enough here of teachers drawing upon that culture in order to help their pupils to a livelier sense of the character and quality of particular works. That culture must of course include scholarship, without which all talk of 'giving the reader priority and not the text' is worthless. If you want to be confident of your response to Chaucer or Pope there are (as Gillian Spraggs and Paul Dean make clear) things you need to know about the literary and social conventions in the work of those writers. Examiners of course complain of the 'clumsy use of background material, biographical, historical, political'. The challenge is to introduce the relevant material at points where it will sensitise rather than displace response.

Such teaching is 'practical criticism' of a direct kind. The comparisons and contrasts that Ian Brinton weaves into his teaching of Edward Thomas's poems; Paul Dean's comparative work on Donne's and Pope's 'translations' of Chaucer—these are concrete ways of introducing students to the history and culture of the language. At times, of course, getting our bearings within that culture may well be an enterprise in which, in varying degrees, we are learning with our pupils. John Haddon with *As You Like It*, Sue Hills with Hopkins' poems, Michael Williams with *The Color Purple*—all begin from a position where, certainly, they would contest HMI's view that there is nothing 'difficult, mysterious or obscure' about the language of literature. They share many of their doubts and difficulties with their students; they are open to correction and to the revaluation of the work in question, but they do not for a moment abandon their claim to lead their students in what, as experienced readers, seem to them the most profitable directions.

Such openness can be uncomfortable, for it includes not only the possibility that our view of a text may change (see David Huband on Jane Austen) but that our attempts to 'get the attraction to seize on' our pupils may coincide with the fading of the book's attraction for ourselves (see G. L. Gibbs on *Catch-22*). Since it is an openness not only to the particular work under study but to life and culture, the teaching (if it goes above the level of dictated notes) will indeed be criticism in action. All teachers are practical critics, good or bad. James, as usual, goes to the heart of the matter; 'It is hard to say whether the literary critic is more called upon to understand or to feel. It is certain that he will accomplish little unless he can feel acutely'. Which is the main reason why we have to say that no book on the teaching of literature can offer a blueprint or a battery of techniques. Who knows when we may be

confronted by a feeling that, perhaps, we ought not to be teaching
Larkin or John Osborne at all? (questions raised by Bryan Robson
and David Walton).

At a time when the general educational and cultural climate is
in so many ways hostile to the arts it is important to insist on their
humanising power, and to do so on the right grounds. As we have
seen, there is an influential current of thought in which works of
the imagination (like the academic subject 'English' itself) are seen
as little more than forms of conditioning, themselves conditioned
by views of which we may or may not approve. In such a view the
teaching of literature becomes instrumental in the way evidently
favoured by Terry Eagleton. Socialist and feminist critics, says
Eagleton, are at one with liberal humanist critics in wishing to
discuss literature 'in ways which will deepen, enrich and extend
our lives'. The difference is 'that they wish to point out that such
deepening and enriching entails the transformation of a society
divided by class and gender'.[31] Seamus Heaney deals with the
temptations of such misplaced earnestness in his recently published
collection of essays *The Government of the Tongue*: 'that vitality
and insouciance of lyric poetry, its relish of its own inventiveness,
its pleasuring strain always comes under threat when poetry remem-
bers that its self-gratification must be perceived as a kind of affront
to a world preoccupied with its own imperfections, pains and
catastrophes'. The contributors to the present volume would (as I
hope the contents prove) share his conviction that 'poetry is its
own reality and no matter how much a poet may concede to the
corrective pressures of social, moral, political and historical reality,
the ultimate fidelity must be to the demands and promise of the
artistic event'.[32]

References

1. Italo Calvino, 'Why Read the Classics', in *The Literature Machine*, Secker and
Warburg 1987, p. 125.
2. Henry James, *The Critical Muse: Selected Literary Criticism*, edited by Roger
Gard, Penguin 1987. All subsequent quotations from James are from this
Selection.
3. Seamus Heaney, 'The God in the Tree, in *Preoccupations*, Faber 1980, p. 184.
4. John Coulson, *Religion and Imagination*, Oxford 1981, p. 70.
5. Matthew Arnold, 'The Literary Influence of Academies' in *The Portable Matthew Arnold*, edited by Lionel Trilling, New York The Viking Press 1956, p.
271.
6. A. Quiller-Couch, 'On the Use of Masterpieces' in *On the Art of Reading*,
Cambridge 1917, p. 200.
7. John Barth, *Writers at Work volume 7*, edited by George Plimpton, Penguin
1988, p. 232.
8. Roger Shattuck, 'How to Rescue Literature', in *The Innocent Eye*, Farrar,
Strauss and Giroux, 1984, p. 313.
9. For instance, Terry Eagleton, *Literary Theory, An Introduction*, Basil

Blackwell, 1983; Chris Baldick, *The Social Mission of English Criticism*, 1848–1932, Oxford, 1983.
10. J. Batsleer, T. Davies, R. O'Rourke, C. Weedon, *Re-writing English*, Methuen New Accents Series, 1985, p. 148.
11. Len Masterman, *Teaching About Television*, Macmillan 1981, p. 18.
12. NATE Post 14 Committee, *English A-level in Practice*, 1988, p. 9.
13. M. Jones and A. West (ed), *Learning Me Your Language*, Mary Glasgow Publications 1988, p. 196.
14. *English A-Level in practice*, p. 27.
15. G. Holderness (ed), *The Shakespeare Myth*, Manchester University Press 1988, pp. 146, 152.
16. R. Wellek, *The Attack on Literature*, Harvester 1982, p. 22.
17. *English A-Level in practice*, p. 30.
18. Ibid., p. 6.
19. Ibid., p. 30.
20. Secondary Examinations Council, *Guide for Teachers of English*, 1986, p. 9.
21. James Gribble, *Literary Education: a Revaluation*, Cambridge, 1983, p. 158.
22. George Eliot, *Selections from George Eliot's Letters*, edited by Gordon Haight, Yale University Press, 1985, p. 318.
23. Seamus Heaney, 'Canticles to the Earth', in *Preoccupations*, p. 190.
24. GCE Examining Boards, *Common Cores at A Level*, 1983.
25. HMI, *A Survey of the Teaching of 'A' Level English in 20 Sixth Forms in Comprehensive Schools*, 1986. See J. Florance and R. Gill, 'The Inspectors Inspected', *Use of English* Autumn 1987. The Article is reprinted in *My Native English*, edited by R. Knight and I. Robinson, Brynmill Press, 1988.
26. Kathleen Raine, *Yeats the Initiate*, Allen and Unwin, 1986, p. 440.
27. Seamus Heaney, 'Belfast', in *Preoccupations*, p. 34.
28. Stephen Spender, Bernard Malamud, Gabriel Marquez, *Writers at Work*, volume 6, edited by George Plimpton, Penguin, 1985, pp. 71, 157, 319.
29. Anthony Thwaite, 'The Guardian', September 27, 1988.
30. Bill Greenwell, *Alternatives at English A Level*, NATE, 1988.
31. Terry Eagleton, p. 210.
32. Seamus Heaney, *The Government of the Tongue*, Faber, 1988, pp. 99, 101.

CHAUCER: *THE WIFE OF BATH'S PROLOGUE AND TALE*

GILLIAN SPRAGGS

What are we to make of the Wife of Bath? Racy, irresistible portrait of a common woman of the Middle Ages? Or monstrous caricature, a concatenation of misogynistic clichés, relieved by flashes of believable personality? I believe that the truth is much closer to the second of these descriptions than the first; but to recognise that this is the case certainly does not have to detract from the appreciation of a text which has been justly celebrated as a literary *tour de force*.

One of the major pitfalls of literary study is succumbing to the temptation to assimilate unfamiliar forms to those with which we are best acquainted: specifically, in this context, to read Chaucer as a kind of primitive novelist. To interpret the *Wife of Bath's Prologue* as though it were intended as a representative picture of everyday life among mediaeval folk, still less to analyse the 'characterisation' of the Wife as though she were a figure in a realistic novel, is to fail to understand the tradition within which Chaucer is writing, and his real achievement within it. It also leads to an unbalanced concentration on the *Prologue*, at the expense of the *Tale*, an imbalance encouraged the more by the fact that the latter belongs unmistakably to a genre, the short fairy tale for adults, which today is highly unfashionable, at least among literary critics.

Of course, the Wife is a 'character', and a wonderful piece of work she is; but we should never allow the sheer volubility, the use of vulgar invective and of exclamations, of rambling asides and of disarmingly proffered confidences, to obscure the fact that the tradition of character-drawing to which she belongs is much closer to that of the stylised set portraits of social types popular in Chaucer's time and for long after, and which are familiar to us today, perhaps, chiefly from Shakespeare's comic countrymen or the stereotyped gallants and grasping misers of Jacobean city comedy, than it is to George Eliot or D. H. Lawrence. Perhaps a useful modern parallel is with a cartoon character such as Andy Capp, or the *Independent*'s irresistibly unpleasant 'yuppie', Alex—highly exaggerated, full of a vigour which is more than life-like;

13

above all, fixed and unchanging—capable of elaboration, but never of development.

I stress this point for several reasons: because I believe that it has been insufficiently emphasised by critics whose work is still influential, because questions inviting the candidate to give an account of the Wife's 'character' still crop up, in various forms, on 'A' level papers, and because I believe that it is often not easily grasped by students whose literary faculties will have been largely trained on texts composed in quite a different tradition. Moreover, as I have said before, it tends to lead to a distorted view of Chaucer's total achievement in the *Prologue and Tale*. At this point, I have to admit to a pronounced personal taste for the literary fairy tale, from the mediaeval 'Breton Lays', through Ruskin, MacDonald and Wilde, to Sylvia Townsend Warner's *Kingdoms of Elfin*. In the context of its genre, I think that the *Wife of Bath's Tale* is a largely unrecognised gem: by turns satirical, mysterious and (as all good fairy stories should be) impeccably moral.

Chaucer's creation of the Wife of Bath depends on a skilful confidence trick. This figure, whose first words are an assertion of her right to speak from 'experience' when it comes to talking of the 'wo that is in marriage', and who sets up her own experience against the 'auctoritee' of the written text, has, in fact, been deftly concocted from a whole range of textual and traditional materials, 'authorities', available to Chaucer and bearing on the nature of women. The most obvious example is the lengthy passage adapted from St Jerome's *Epistle Against Jovinian*, and borrowed by him in turn from a now lost satire against marriage by the Greek writer Theophrastus. More diffuse is the influence of Jean de Meun, thirteenth-century continuator of the *Roman de la Rose*, whose pronounced misogyny provoked a celebrated literary debate a few years after Chaucer was writing. Much similar borrowing, from a range of different writers, has been traced throughout the *Prologue*; while other material which has gone into the construction of the Wife is less literary, as in the case of the proverb the Wife is made complacently to cite:

Deceite, weping, spinning God hath yive
To wommen kindely, whil that they may live.

The stereotypes of traditional misogyny still find echoes today, in our supposedly 'post-feminist' society: women are vain, untrustworthy, are always moaning, can never keep a secret . . . Does any of this sound familiar?

This material, of course, is entirely male in its origins and outlook. Chaucer is writing as a male intellectual at a time when virtually all intellectuals were not only men but were educated in a tradition dominated by a Church which not only emphasised in its doctrine the peculiar frailty of women, morally and intellectually, but stigmatised them as a snare and a distraction and kept its functionaries (in theory, at least) segregated from everyday contact with the female sex. So much for 'experience'. But when this has been recognised, it needs to be emphasised that Chaucer's relationship with that tradition was not an altogether simple one. After all, he makes his representative married woman exclaim:

> Who peyntede the leon, tel me who?
> By God! if wommen hadde writen stories,
> As clerkes han withinne hire oratories—

the Wife of Bath knows very well whom she has to thank for the unflattering view of women current in mediaeval literature—

> They wolde han writen of men moore wikkednesse
> Than al the mark of Adam may redresse.

But the satire, as so often in Chaucer, works in more than one direction. The Wife of Bath, who responds so hotly to her husbands' accusations, reveals in her own accounts of her behaviour that their complaints are entirely justified; she who protests that monastic writers never have anything good to say about women is a self-confessed embodiment of all their claims.

With all this in view, it is bizarre to find that James Winny, editor of the standard school edition of *The Wife of Bath's Prologue and Tale*, can say in his introduction, evidently quite straight-faced, that

> She observes the working of her feminine instincts with an interest both absorbed and critically detached, setting her own emotional vagaries in the larger context of womanly nature, which she describes with familiar understanding.

He cites, in support of this observation, the Wife of Bath's statement that women always hanker most after what they cannot have. To accept the clichés of a misogynistic tradition as insights into 'womanly nature' is at once unscholarly and offensive.

Somewhere behind Winny's remark seems to be the common notion that the greatest literature is to be valued above all for offering us universal truths about 'life' or 'human nature'. It does not take much reflection to see that literature can never tell us the whole truth about anything, let alone about 'human nature'. What it can show us is something of the ideas and assumptions current at the time it was written, and something of the writer's own relationship with those ideas, whether conformist, critical or heterodox. Some or perhaps all of what a particular text offers on the level of meaning may be seized on by the reader as expressing valid and even important insights; and this is wholly as it should be. It would be entirely regrettable if literary study were either to become dominated by an aridly exclusive preoccupation with form, or be forced into the straitjacket of a rigidly historical approach, with the text viewed as an interesting but irrelevant relic. But our understanding of any text is invariably shaped to a large extent both by the current wisdom of our own times and by the perspectives from which we individually view that wisdom. Arguably, literature is at its most valuable when it leads us to look carefully and critically at a particular orthodoxy. *The Wife of Bath's Prologue* can be read in such a way that it helps to bring misogyny, past and present, into clearer focus. As Winny's statement shows, it can also still be read in a way that I believe is both crass and damaging, as a reinforcement of misogynistic stereotypes. The sustained attack on the morals and mentality of the female sex is no longer in fashion as a literary genre; but we are still heirs to the culture that produced such works.

The Wife of Bath, then, is only a representative figure in the sense that she reflects a masculine consensus, both learned and popular, on the nature of women. Indeed in order to reflect this consensus fully, she is made in one important area to embrace a degree of contradiction. On the one hand, she is portrayed as sexually insatiable, holding her unfortunate husbands in a state of sexual slavery: 'How pitously a-night I made hem swinke!', she gloats. On the other hand, she is apparently well able to withhold her sexual favours when it suits her, and she uses this to manipulate her husbands into giving her her own way:

> Namely abedde hadden they meschaunce:
> Ther wolde I chide, and do hem no plesaunce.

This is the punitive figure of man's bad dream, not a plausibly constructed character. It tells us far more about masculine fears than about the nature of women.

Having said this, it should be recognised, firstly, that Chaucer's satire cuts in more than one direction; secondly, that the Wife of Bath is not, like her literary forerunner, Jean de Meun's Vekke (Duenna) in the *Roman de la Rose*, a merely corrupt figure, a wicked woman, held up for obloquy. The Duenna's account of her career forms a substantial digression in the French poem, along with her advice on love. She exemplifies the seedy old age of a woman of sexually licentious life, and she features as the mouthpiece for a vicious doctrine of selfish and callous exploitation. By contrast, the Wife of Bath is an energetic and engaging disputant in a dramatised debate about how to achieve a lasting accord in marriage. Chaucer is giving comic treatment to a crucial topic, with relevance to the lives of most people, women and men alike. Nor does he allow the men any advantage: Jankin is rather a contemptible figure, a hypocritical young libertine who is happy enough to play around with his master's wife, but who after his master is dead and they are married, adopts the pose of a moralist, and whose academic learning merely teaches him to treat his wife with rancorous contempt. As for the knight in the *Tale*, he is an unsavoury rapist, dependent for his life on the conditional compassion of the Queen and the insight of the 'olde wyf', and in serious need of the lesson which he has learned by the end of the story: what women want most of all is 'maistrie', to invert, in other words, the traditional subordination of women to men.

Why 'maistrie'? Why not equality? The answer lies partly in the rooted assumptions of an age which could not conceive of social structures—or, indeed, the structure of the natural world—in other than hierarchical terms, and whose theologians were capable of offering as grounds for the subordination of women the argument that for convenience' sake, one or the other sex had to be given pre-eminence. But the answer is also to be found in the demands of Chaucer's genres: he was writing a comic monologue linked to a fairy story, not a sober discourse on marriage. Inversion, in its many forms, is a classic pattern in both the comic and romantic modes: the Justice is put in the stocks, the poor lad outwits the giant, the goosegirl becomes a queen. The shifts of power, from the ostensibly powerful to the powerless, the defying of common sense expectations as to outcome (which the genre nevertheless signals us to anticipate) is a crucial part of the pleasure we are invited to feel.

For above all, *The Wife of Bath's Prologue and Tale* is tremendously entertaining. One of the most rewarding aspects of teaching this text is the spontaneous, scandalized laughter it arouses in adolescents who are still struggling to adjust to the demands of reading Middle English. We certainly do not have to accept the Wife of Bath as a wholly convincing portrait in order to enjoy ourselves as she systematically flouts conventional ideals of appropriate womanly behaviour—ideals that are by no means entirely dead. Nor do we have to believe in fairies in order to appreciate the tricky dilemma of the knight in the *Tale*.

For all except a handful of quite exceptional 'A' level students, their Chaucer text is likely to be the only mediaeval literary work they will ever have seen. As a result, the teacher needs to take exceptional care in the initial approach to the poem. To begin with, it is important that before the book is even opened, some insight should be offered into the ideologies and social structures of mediaeval England. Obviously, the starting point must be with what the students know, or think they know, about life in the Middle Ages. In my experience, this is seldom very much, in these days of Combined Humanities, and usually seems to owe more to *Robin of Sherwood* and other television dramas than to historical study.

Three aspects of mediaeval life and thought stand in particular need of explanation: the role of religion and the Church, the position of women (both actual and theoretical), and the social distinction between those of 'gentle' birth, that is ancient aristocratic family, and the rest, the commoners. An understanding of this last is crucial to appreciating the context of the 'olde wyf's' disquisition on 'gentillesse', in the *Tale*. In particular, it is important to explain the very ancient aristocratic assumption that to be superior in birth, specifically to come of parents of 'gentle' or 'noble' rank, was also to be superior in moral terms: an outlook which persisted long after Chaucer's time, and has left many relics embedded still in our language and attitudes, for example in the nuances of meaning found in words like 'mean', 'churlish', 'noble', and in usages like 'Honourable' employed as a title for the offspring of certain sections of the peerage. In attacking this belief, both in *The Wife of Bath's Tale* and elsewhere in his writings, Chaucer was speaking from a completely orthodox Christian standpoint, opposing the doctrine of the Church to the values of the aristocracy. It is not strange that Chaucer, who for all his courtly training and service was not an aristocrat but came from a family of successful London businessmen—from a background, in fact, not too dissimilar to that of the Wife of Bath, that leading entrepreneur of the cloth trade—should have vigorously argued the case for 'gentillesse' as a quality revealed in behaviour, not in inherited position.

There is an excellent account of mediaeval ideas about women in the first chapter of Eileen Power's *Mediaeval Women*, which is also invaluable as a source of information about women's lives. Scholarly but very accessible, this book may be usefully recommended to students. Derek Brewer's *Chaucer and his World* is another book in which impeccable scholarship is retailed in a lively and enjoyable manner; it offers an account of Chaucer's career in the context of the social life of his times, and is splendidly illustrated. Pictures are very important in helping students to conjure up in their imaginations the physical world of late fourteenth-century England. A raid on the school or public library for books on mediaeval art is helpful here; I have also found that my collection of postcards from art galleries and museums can be invaluable. The famous miniatures of the individual pilgrims from the Ellesmere MS of the *Canterbury Tales* are obviously a splendid visual stimulus, if reproductions can be obtained.

As *The Wife of Bath's Prologue and Tale* forms only a small section of a much larger work of art, it is obviously necessary to give some preliminary account of *The Canterbury Tales* as a whole, and of the framework of the pilgrimage. There is an excellent chapter on pilgrims and pilgrimages in J. J. Jusserand's *English Wayfaring Life in the Middle Ages*, a book for which I have a great deal of affection, a classic of social history, now nearing its centenary but still not wholly superseded. I do not like recommending criticism (as opposed to works of social history) to students before the text itself has been read, at least in part, since I think that it is likely to interfere with the spontaneity and individuality of their response, so I will postpone suggesting critical texts for a few more paragraphs.

The Wife of Bath's Prologue begins rather unpromisingly: we are precipitated into a debate, evidently ongoing, on 'experience' and 'auctoritee'. We do not know how Chaucer meant to link the Wife's opening speech into the *Tales* as a whole; as it stands, it is at the beginning of a fragment which also includes the tales of the Friar and the Summoner. A further difficulty is the fact that the term 'auctoritee' is being used in what to modern ears is a rather specialised sense, somewhat peripheral to the usages of the word 'authority' common today. Rather than beginning here, then, I recommend starting by looking at a few selected parts of the *General Prologue*, filling in the rest with brief paraphrases in modern English. Sections which can usefully be read include parts of the description of the Friar, some understanding of whose characteristics is essential for appreciating the opening to the *Tale*, the description of the Wife herself, and the Host's proposal of the story-telling contest. I have not found it necessary to burden students in advance with much information about grammar; they quickly pick up what they need to know as they go along. Pronunciation does need some specific discussion; in particular, they need to have their attention drawn to the fact that in many cases final 'e' was not then mute as it is now, as unless they realise this they will be unable to make sense of the metre. The standard school edition by Winny includes a brief note on pronunciation. I also consulted the fuller account in F. N. Robinson's Oxford edition of Chaucer's *Works*, which I found invaluable for reference purposes. This has recently been thoroughly revised, and reissued as *The Riverside Chaucer*, edited by Larry D. Benson.

Once they have begun to gain confidence in reading Chaucerian English, it is time that students started to prepare a translation in advance of each lesson of the part of the text to be studied. The only way to ensure that this work is done properly by each of them is to make them take in turns the task of expounding the text to the rest of the group, ignoring alike both the wails of the easily-discouraged and the objections of those students who persist in adopting the self-destructive attitude that it is your job, not theirs, to do the work necessary to 'get them through' their 'A' level.

Discussion of the literary qualities of the text is bound to focus initially on the characteristics of the central figure. I encouraged my students to look carefully at the way she is constructed: the effective use of particular detail and of the skilful imitation of the language and patterns of everyday speech to flesh out a stereotype composed of hoary clichés. Their first piece of written work apart from translation was set on this topic; preparatory discussion in class took place after reading the *Prologue* and before tackling the *Tale*.

Among critical texts, I particularly commend to teachers and students alike Derek Brewer's *An Introduction to Chaucer*, which offers an excellent discussion of *The Canterbury Tales* and includes several very useful pages on *The Wife of Bath's Prologue and Tale*. Jill Mann's *Chaucer and Mediaeval Estates Satire* is a more specialised study and focuses on the *General Prologue*, finding its source material in earlier mediaeval literature about the different ranks and occupations in society. It contains a useful discussion of the Wife of Bath considered in relation to traditional anti-female stereotypes. A sound general introduction to the critical study of mediaeval texts is A. C. Spearing's *Criticism and Mediaeval Poetry*, which does not, however, include any specific consideration of *The Wife of Bath's Prologue and Tale*. Particularly helpful are a discussion of the effect on mediaeval literature of composition for oral performance, and an account of mediaeval attitudes towards the use of borrowed material.

Study of the *Tale* needs to be prefaced by some examination of the genres of romance and fairy tale, and their popularity in Chaucer's society. Their claims to be taken seriously may be upheld by pointing out the parallels with modern traditions of speculative story-telling in the shape of science fiction and Tolkienesque fantasy. I may add that I have no sympathy with critics who find the *Tale* an inappropriate story for the Wife of Bath to tell. There is plenty of evidence that the mediaeval bourgeoisie enjoyed tales of romance at least as much as members of the knightly classes to whom romance heroes conventionally belonged; moreover, the Wife of Bath is a firm believer in love, and in living happily ever after—just as she and Jankin did, after they had sorted out their differences. Furthermore, had the Wife been allocated some scurrilous tale of sexual intrigue, like the *fabliaux* recounted by the

Miller, Reeve and Shipman, the overall structure at this point in *The Caterbury Tales* would have suffered sadly from a loss of contrast: after the Wife's own personal history of domestic strife and duplicity, more of the same could only have been wearisome.

When considering in more detail the ideas about women and marriage found in the text, I found it very helpful to borrow of set of Bibles from the RE department and take the class through some of the passages cited by the Wife, examining the uses (and misuses) to which she puts them. I also found that a clearer appreciation of the context and tone of *The Wife of Bath's Prologue* was stimulated by a look at the writing of one of the very few mediaeval women whose own reactions to the misogynistic tradition are still available to us. Christine de Pisan was a younger contemporary of Chaucer, an Italian woman who was brought up at the French court. Widowed at twenty-five, she turned to writing to support herself and her three small children, achieving considerable recognition and success. In several of her works, Christine set out to defend her sex against the attacks of literary misogynists. She had a particular dislike of the work of Jean de Meun, author of the heavily satirical continuation to the *Roman de la Rose* and prominent influence on Chaucer, and she criticised his writing in the course of a famous polemical correspondence.

The most accessible and useful of Christine's works in the present context is *The Book of the City of Ladies*, recently made available in a paperback translation. Christine begins by describing how she started to read a book on the subject of women, but finding that it was full of insulting lies, put it down. As she was wondering why it was that so many men felt impelled to write about women with such hostility and contempt, she began to feel depressed and full of self-hatred: 'for I detested myself and the entire feminine sex, as though we were monstrosities in nature' (I.1.1). At this point, Christine has a vision: three crowned ladies, Reason, Rectitude ('Correct Thinking') and Justice, appear before her and tell her to disregard the evil things that are said against women, and to build 'the City of Ladies' on 'the Field of Letters'—in other words, to write a defence of her sex. The rest of the book consists of a dialogue with each in turn in which common misogynistic clichés are exposed and refuted.

The Book of the City of Ladies is best used in short extracts, after a brief explanation of the allegorical machinery: the book is too lengthy and the allegorical mode is too alienating to the unaccustomed modern reader for it to be recommended to students for solitary reading. I found it was useful for broadening students' acquaintance with mediaeval literature and habits of thought, and particularly for encouraging them to look more critically at the way in which the character of the Wife has been constructed. It is enjoyable and thought-provoking to speculate how Christine de Pisan would have reacted to reading *The Wife of Bath's Prologue and Tale.*

One of the most exciting inquiries with regard to this text lies in exploring the sources and nature of the comedy: to put it simply, why do we laugh when we do? Do we laugh at the Wife, or with her? Or both? Is the *Prologue* simply uproarious, or does it strike other notes? If so, do these deepen or detract from the comedy? Pursuing such investigations takes us into the heart of the qualities of great comic writing. Moelwyn Merchant's slim volume on *Comedy* is by no means the best of the series to which it belongs, Methuen's *The Critical Idiom*, but it can be recommended as a starting point to the interested student.

Obviously it is desirable that students should have an opportunity to form an impression for themselves of the overall structure and the variety of *The Canterbury Tales.* Realistically, one must face the fact that only a very exceptional student will choose to read further in Middle English. Nevill Coghill's translation of the whole work, available in Penguin, may be recommended as readable and reasonably close to the original: but not until the *Prologue and Tale* have been read completely through in class; otherwise some students will try to use it as a crib. Another useful aid which perhaps needs to be held back until at least part of the book has been studied, if not the whole, is a recording of the text read in Middle English. A two disc set of *The Wife of Bath's Prologue and Tale*, read by Prunella Scales and Richard Bebb, is available from Argo Records, who also have on their list recordings of various other parts of *The Canterbury Tales.*

Ironically, or so it would seem, this essentially misogynistic text is one of the books which I have had most pleasure out of teaching. More important, perhaps, though no doubt not unrelated, was the evident enjoyment of most of the students. One or two dissidents clearly resented the sheer hard slog which was necessary at the start, as the class came to grips with an unfamiliar syntax and archaic vocabulary. Others obviously saw these oddities as an intriguing challenge. Most were, I think, surprised at how relatively quickly they found themselves at ease reading Middle English. Clearly, the Wife's sexual frankness was one factor in stirring students' enthusiasm. Like most people, nowadays as in Chaucer's own time, adolescents enjoy smut. Her reference to 'queynte' shocked some students initially, until I pointed out that the taboo on this word dates from more recent times than Chaucer's. The Wife is outspoken, but never merely crude; to Chaucer's audience, she would have sounded blunt, but not offensive.

The themes which Chaucer treats in *The Wife of Bath's Prologue and Tale* are weighty and enduring. It is one measure of his brilliance that the humour with which he handles them is still largely accessible to us, five centuries later, after many vicissitudes of language and taste. In the end, it is her resolute determination to enjoy herself which makes us feel that the Wife is such good company; to let her have the last word, as is only right and proper: 'But yet to be right mirie wol I fonde.'

References

1. Texts

Larry D. Benson, ed., *The Riverside Chaucer.* (1987) Oxford University Press; Oxford, 1988.
F. N. Robinson, ed., *The Works of Geoffrey Chaucer.* Oxford University Press; London, 1957.
James Winny, ed., *The Wife of Bath's Prologue and Tale.* (1965) Cambridge University Press; Cambridge, 1984.

2. Other Works

Derek Brewer, *Chaucer and his World.* Eyre Methuen; London, 1978.
Derek Brewer, *An Introduction to Chaucer.* Longman; London, 1984.
Geoffrey Chaucer, *The Canterbury Tales*, trans. Neville Coghill. (1951) Penguin Books; Harmondsworth, 1987.
J. J. Jusserand, *English Wayfaring Life in the Middle Ages*, trans. Lucy Toulmin Smith. (1889) Methuen; London, 1961.
Guillaume de Lorris and Jean de Meun, *The Romance of the Rose*, trans. Harry W. Robbins. Dutton; New York, 1962.
Jill Mann, *Chaucer and Mediaeval Estates Satire.* Cambridge University Press; Cambridge, 1973.
Moelwyn Merchant, *Comedy.* The Critical Idiom. (1972) Methuen; London, 1980.
Christine de Pizan, *The Book of the City of Ladies.* trans. Earl Jeffrey Richards. (1982) Pan Books; London, 1983.
Eileen Power, *Medieval Women*, ed. M. M. Postan. Cambridge University Press; Cambridge, 1975.
A. C. Spearing, *Criticism and Medieval Poetry.* (1964) Edward Arnold; London, 1972.

3. Recordings

The Canterbury Tales: The Wife of Bath's Prologue and Tale, read by Prunella Scales and Richard Bebb. Argo Records; ZPL 1212/1213.
The Canterbury Tales: Prologue, read by Neville Coghill, Norman Davis, John Burrow. Argo Records; PLP 1001.

SHAKESPEARE: EXPLORING THE IDEA OF LOVE IN *AS YOU LIKE IT*

JOHN HADDON

'Romantic love is a state of facts.'   —Charles Williams

It doesn't ensure automatic results if the teacher has some degree of inward possession of the text, but it at least helps him in finding (coming to know) his own bearings. Somehow *As You Like It* had never *occurred* to me. Nor do I know how that occurrence can be brought about. (Yet it is that occurrence one hopes will come about in one's students.) I approached the first lesson, then, at something of a disadvantage. Also it was a difficult term; a number of things had gone wrong departmentally and I needed time for sorting them out. So I began by setting up a task and withdrawing, only checking periodically to see that the work was still growing and setting the class (of nine girls) on to the subsequent stages. They had already read the play during the previous holiday. I wanted something that would ensure a pretty complete knowledge of the text and also some penetration of its suggestiveness, its possible range or depth or resonance of meaning (about which I had myself very little idea). As it happened, I set them two tasks, intended to be complementary.

First (since I had been reading Richard Adams' collection *Teaching Shakespeare* and the idea had caught my eye) I asked the class to cast the play from the pupils and staff of the school—insisting, of course, that they should be able to justify their choices from, as we say, the text. (Emphasis here squarely—and potentially misleadingly—on 'character'.) Initially intended as an exercise at once introductory and holding, this grew into a sequence of work that took some weeks. I next invited them to find locations—the Court and the Forest of Arden—in or around school (nearby Tutbury Castle proved irresistible); then to reduce the play to a sequence of photographic 'stills' that captured (encapsulated) the main action. (Emphasis pretty much on plot, and begging the question of at what level 'action' in this play might properly be said to subsist—but I hoped something might come up.) Each 'still' had to be carefully composed. Two photo sessions followed, the class having contacted their 'cast' and directed the photographer minutely. Finally, to go with each picture they had to select a fragment or fragments of text. By this time I had decided that the whole thing would culminate in a display.

However, a persistent worry throughout this, as I have parenthetically indicated, was that while this work might secure a good knowledge of the surface of the play it might also fix that knowledge at a superficial plot-and-character (shall we say, pre-'A'-) level, rather than have been preparatory. So I introduced at some point—quite early if I remember correctly—a second project for the girls to work on individually, without consultation. (Here I was influenced by the approaches of Bill Greenwell, approaches that I found interesting but about which I had—and have—reservations.) I asked them each to produce, by an agreed date, an object of their own devising that *metaphorically* represented *As You Like It*. Using these two approaches I hoped that they would not only have done adequate groundwork but also provided hints for future discussion/development/direction.

These visual metaphors, when unveiled, proved interesting and varied, although inclined to the allegorical—some kind of literalism—rather than the metaphorical. Lesley had made a mask (for disguise), heart-shaped (for love) divided in halves: one sad (banishment), one happy (comedy, joy). Sarah, thinking similarly, produced a hat (worn for disguise), divided to show court (greed, intrigue, falsity) and forest (faithfulness, friendship). But she had thought beyond a simple half and half: from the top of the hat leaves grew from the court's yellow ('as the characters . . . begin to "turn over new leaves"'), and beside them grew an open hand, 'symbolising friendship and purity once again'. Hands, crossed and open in reconciling acceptance, were central to Lisa's design. Emma made a heart, broken, from which grew the horns of a jester's hat, the whole bright red and yellow.

Thinking rather differently, Heather brought a cubic jigsaw puzzle in white plastic, a heart at its centre: the Love Puzzle, 'a game in which the pieces have to be fitted together in the correct places in order for the puzzle to be completed—just as the relationships had to be identified and recognised before the play concludes . . . the hole in the centre of the heart represents the bitterness and deception involved within the play'.

Alison, with extraordinary patience, produced a diagrammatic representation of the growth of the relationships in the play, each character's fortunes traced painstakingly in coloured wire, the whole a complex emblem of *As You Like It*. The paired lines reached their destination as they joined in the shape of little hearts. (But also, they looked like bums. 'Very appropriate for that play', said someone when I mentioned it. I wouldn't want to dwell too much on the hearts/bums coincidence, or declare myself of

Touchstone's party, but I did feel the need to point out, when the class later commented that the play's romantic love-at-first-sight is very different from Touchstone's 'realism', that 'they have made a pair of stairs to marriage, which they will climb incontinent, or else be incontinent before marriage' is not a million miles removed from 'We must be married or we must live in bawdry'. The *nature* of the difference, that's what's worth pursuing. Hearts don't exclude, but nor do they collapse into, bums in Shakespeare's romantic comedy. The enthusiasm of these couples for each other includes (and may only just *contain*) *desire*. Part of what *is* wonderful about Shakespeare's language of love . . . but I anticipate.)

Perhaps the wittiest metaphor was Caroline's, which represented *As You Like It* as a tin of trifle, 'Lightly concocted from fruits of the forest'—especially passion fruit—and containing 'artificial flavouring', decked out with a mask and a party hat. 'Although', Caroline wrote in the brief notes to accompany the metaphors in our display, 'a lot of genuine emotion is expressed, the atmosphere of the play and the traditional happy ending suggest that *As You Like It* is not to be taken VERY seriously!' Well, not too seriously, obviously. But this became my question, my point of entry: how serious is *As You Like It*; how is *As You Like It* serious?

While the girls seemed to enjoy the work and find it interesting, my nagging doubt remained, that after all we had not yet met the play, as Shakespeare's work lives in its language, not in story and theme apart from it. I didn't know how much the very language of the play had entered into their thinking about it. It still hadn't, much, into mine. The only previous time I had used a pictorial approach had been late in a study of *The Tempest*, after several conventional essays had been written, and there it had worked well. I think that the approach has its uses, but that it must always be balanced by others. Part of the difficulty of judging how successful something of this kind has been is in not having been privy to the discussions that took place, or to the thoughts of individuals. I am therefore extremely grateful to Alison, who, after reading my first draft of this essay, provided me with some written observations.

In her view my fears were unjustified. The exercise *had* been seen as preparatory, and the composing of the 'stills', the designing of the final display, and the metaphors introduced a number of issues that were explored in depth later. Alison felt that they had 'recognised the importance of language although it took time to be brought out as a topic of study', and that this awareness led them 'to what I saw as fruitful discussion later on'. Clearly useful discussion went on out of class—Alison had argued with Caroline about her 'trifle' comment, for instance. I find revealing Alison's admission that

> the majority of us felt that this pictorial approach was a tangent from the 'proper'
> work; most of us had this idea that 'A' level should not be 'fun', and I don't
> think we were consciously aware of *learning* anything, although later discussions
> clearly demonstrated that we *had* learnt a lot from the exercise. . . . Our doubts
> came mainly before we had actually started on the exercise; as it progressed they
> were removed. I don't think any of us would now say that we didn't find it
> valuable.

Personally, she had found the metaphor work the most rewarding—
both her own and the discussion of others'.

The visual metaphors, for the most part bright in primary colours,
uncomplicated in design, embody a view of *As You Like It* as
cheerful, straightforward, not to be taken very seriously, and above
all *pleasant*. I felt strongly that I wanted to put that to the test; not
necessarily to insinuate darker elements, (it was only later that we
began to feel that they might be present, that the oppressiveness
in the opening scenes might be more than notional; although
Heather, note, meaning to or not, placed bitterness and emptiness
at the *centre*: a mistake, I think), but to weigh properly the play's
pleasantness—in particular, the nature and the quality of the love
in it, and the question of realism/reality.

We spent a lesson comparing *As You Like It* to *The Tempest*,
which they had studied previously. We noted the common themes
(love, deceit, banishment, usurpation, restoration) but the class
argued that in *The Tempest* these themes had weight and that the
sense of reality was greater. In particular, they felt that in *As You
Like It* the love-at-first-sight and the ending were unrealistic, or,
as Emma more appropriately(?) put it, 'not real'. (But why should
the same not be said of *The Tempest*? Here I did get their at least
notional assent to the suggestion that whatever the difference was,
it must be a matter of the language. Perhaps I should have insisted
on a closer comparison of love in the two plays.) During this
discussion Caroline's 'trifle' view became more dominant: *As You
Like It* is delightful, and delightful = insignificant, i.e. carrying no
meaning worth serious consideration. We (I) hit a problem with
'serious', as it was felt to be synonymous with 'heavy, solemn' (one
thing we might learn from *As You Like It* is that it needn't
be). Arguing with an essay by Lisa I produced a definition from
Chambers: 'in earnest: not to be taken lightly', but I doubt if I was
very persuasive, given the feeling that 'lightly' is just how things
are taken in this play. I wanted to be able to show how *lightness*
and *depth* can go together in the play's finest moments; or rather,
I wanted the girls to find that out (as we say) for themselves.

After further discussion, I asked them to write on love in the
play, giving not one essay title but ten, inviting them to pick up

and explore suggestions from as few or as many as they wished, but as thoroughly as possible. The questions invited consideration of how deep the love in the play is, to what extent it is merely conventional, whether it is merely mocked, seen to be ridiculous, whether the marriages are an absurd plot expedient . . . Among the questions I included three that roughly expressed the view that I was coming to hold.

—'*As You Like It* provides a number of perspectives on romantic love; but they are ordered in such a way that romantic love, although subjected to mockery and shrewd criticism, is finally vindicated.' Discuss.
—'True love in *As You Like It* may be light, but it is also strong.' Discuss.
—'Love in *As You Like It* must be serious; for Rosalind is in love, and she is serious.' Discuss.

It was interesting to note that although most insisted that the play was unrealistic and unreal (Heather pointing out that this 'does not have to be a criticism' and that a play can be *satisfying* without being realistic) they brought realistic understandings to bear in some of their readings; that is to say, they read psychologically, with insufficient regard for convention and poetry. For instance, some said that Orlando couldn't *really* love Rosalind, or he would have seen through her disguise, and that if Rosalind really loved Orlando she would have revealed her identity. And they psychologised Touchstone, arguing that his reductive view of marriage is his defensive reaction to having been hurt in love. By whom? Well, by Jane Smile. But surely she is a transparent fiction? In that passage (II.iv.41–59) Touchstone is mocking emptily; he has no title among 'we that are true lovers'. Here, I argued, psychology—this kind of psychology, anyway—works against the text's suggestions. Well then, if not by Jane Smile, by Rosalind, who is unaware of his love, and whom he can never have. So it will have to be Audrey. (Poor Audrey. And poor William, who for a long while I thought the best character in the play, with his wonderfully civil 'God rest you merry, sir' to the odious barrage he gets from Touchstone.) Several also felt that Celia fell in love with Orlando—a matter, I suppose, of symmetry. (It's fair to remark that this might be a response to a formal element as much as a misplaced psychology.) The two girls are so close, and there is the young man, so why shouldn't they both . . .? However, 'as Rosalind is the more dominant of the pair, she went ahead and won his heart. Celia had to accept second best and that is why I think she married Oliver' (Emma). (But Rosalind did nothing, other than to be there, to win Orlando's heart.) The textual evidence adduced was:

Rosalind. The little strength that I have, I would it were with you
Celia. And mine to eke out hers.

But that needn't at all be an expansion of love in the sense that desires marriage as an outcome; it could be just concern, on both their parts. (Rosalind may say more than Celia hears.) A question we might have considered more is the exact point at which Rosalind falls in love. But falling in love like that, it seems, has to be explained, or it is unsatisfactory in some way—some find it hard to accept the love *as love*.

Love at first sight may be a convention, but 'We cannot begin to understand a particular convention without referring to the fact of nature of which it aims to make sense' (Carol McMillan). Sarah, expressing a common opinion, wrote 'The days are over when love at first sight takes place'. *Are* they? I find that unconvincing. More interestingly, Rebecca argued that the attraction between Rosalind and Orlando is 'so sudden that we can only presume it is lust, as love can only occur when a person's character is fully known and admired. These two people hardly know each other'. But I don't think that that is an adequate characterisation of the moment (unless desire is always and only lust). There's a paragraph in Coleridge's notes on the first act of *The Tempest* that is helpful to consider in this respect—a better psychology of love at first sight:

> . . . it appears to me, that in all cases of real love, it is at one moment that it takes place. The moment may have been prepared by previous esteem, admiration, or even affection,—yet love seems to require a momentary act of volition, by which a tacit bond of devotion is imposed . . .

Further, I suggested that perhaps the notion of love-at-first-sight working here involves the idea that in the moment *the entirety of the beloved* becomes apparent—that love is a mode of complete knowledge. (I wouldn't yet want to go along with the view that what Orlando sees in Rosalind is the Platonic Beauty—a view argued by John Vyvyan. I had intended to discuss this view with the class but never got round to it. They had responded with interest to Colin Still's allegorical reading of *The Tempest*, so might have found Vyvyan persuasive.) If something like this view of the convention *as used here by Shakespeare* is correct, the notion, introduced by Ruth and Rebecca, that Rosalind's love *progresses* or *deepens* as the play goes on is mistaken, as the love is given and complete; we would have to talk instead of her realising more fully the extent of that love she already has—which 'hath an unknown bottom, like the bay of Portugal'. (We see here her willingness to see, to enjoy, what is ridiculous in her love, or how her love makes her ridiculous, without for a moment doubting or discrediting it. The wonder of this love can't be had apart from its absurdity.)

'The love is unnatural and cannot be taken seriously' (Lesley); 'personally I feel the love is not as deep as it seems' (Emma); *but* 'it is obvious that the love runs deep' (Lisa). Some, even given doubts about the conventions, felt able to accept the love. Ruth, for instance, asked pointedly why we *shouldn't* accept it:

> Rosalind and Orlando say constantly that they love each other. Should we have to doubt them? . . . if they are not mistaken and they both mean what they say—if they do, then I see their love as being serious.

This raises the difficult question of how we *know* if they mean what they say (see Philip Edwards' thought-provoking essay 'The Declaration of Love'). It is a matter of the quality of what they say, or do we assume as a donnée that the love is real? This question, which I would have liked us to have tried to get to the bottom of, is a point at which we stuck several times.

But we did move on to look (although not enough) at the styles of love in the play, and at the play's criticism of those styles. We studied Phebe's mockery of the conventional love language of Silvius' protestations, and noted the unfairness of that mockery, its ungenerous refusal (or failure) to see the facts of nature on which the conventions are founded. (Of course such utterances can be *merely* conventional, but she doesn't give him the benefit of the doubt.) And we saw her tumble at once into love and the conventional expression of it, to be mocked in her turn.

At this point, wondering if I ought, I read the class a bit of Eagleton:

> Shakespearean comedy is acutely aware that characters in love are simultaneously at their most 'real' and 'unreal', most true and most feigning. Love is the ultimate self-definition, the most precious and unique mode of being; yet it is always intolerably hackneyed and banal, something that millions of people have done before and millions more will do again. To say 'I love you', as Jonathan Culler points out, is always at some level a quotation; in its very moment of absolute, original value, the self stumbles across nothing but other people's lines, finds itself handed a meticulously detailed script to which it must slavishly conform . . .

There's a lot to be sorted out there, but apparently it caused little interest and I dropped it quickly. However, I was quite wrong about this, as Alison's note makes clear:

> I can still remember the idea of [love as] quotation and we were all pretty stunned by the realisation . . . although it may not have *directly* caused 'English' interest.

A missed opportunity, perhaps. But then some useful—perhaps sometimes the best—discussion may take place without, and beyond the ken of, the teacher. Instead we went on to look at Rosalind as a critic of love—at Ganymede.

The questions I asked them to consider were: How are we to take Ganymede's misogyny and 'realism'? How does it differ from Touchstone's? What of love survives her criticism? But above all, why is Rosalind doing it—or, rather, what is it that she is doing?

And how is it that she is able to do it? The prose in which she denigrates love is marvellously fluent and expressive: does Rosalind have the resources to say those things in that way? Can those things be said in that way and not be meant? What is the relationship between Rosalind and Ganymede? (I suggested, only a little flippantly: Ganymede is Rosalind on holiday.)

I certainly don't know the answer to any of these questions with any confidence; I am pleasantly baffled, beyond a feeling that there's no malice in it and several wonderful lines ('No, faith, die by attorney . . . men have died from time to time and worms have eaten them, but not for love'), and that somehow Rosalind's love not only survives but lives in Ganymede's criticism. Obviously questions of psychology versus—no, in relation to—convention need to be worked out, and to do so is not easy.

So I was delighted to read the essays that followed. Still largely working on 'realistic/psychological' principles, they had a notable perceptiveness and maturity of expression, as in, for example, Caroline's neatly balanced appraisal of the place of Rosalind/ Ganymede's deception:

> . . . the plot demands it while the mood of the play and Rosalind's character allow for it.

However, Emma's observation that

> . . . deep down I think it hurts her to have to keep this disguise between them; she would have much rather revealed herself and married him, but I think she wanted to be absolutely sure of him before she made the final commitment

while thoughtful and well expressed does, I think, reveal a weakness of this way of thinking here—where does this pain show *at all* in Rosalind's lines? A much more persuasive reading of the same kind, and finely expressed, is Heather's:

> . . . she shows a strength unseen in her familiar part as a woman, implying that the portrayal of masculinity helps to develop her own characteristics, almost as if she is now able to see the weakness in women from a distance, rather than being a part . . . by using Ganymeade she is creating a greater distance between the characters of Rosalind and Ganymede, men and women, whilst at the same time questioning, or maybe discovering for the first time various aspects of love;

and magnificently:

> . . . by providing answers and objections which defend his affections [she is] confirming her hopes, not Ganymede's suspicions.

I also liked Sarah's comment that

> . . . she is able to get to know him as himself rather than through the mask of airs and graces that a courtship could provoke.

After all, Orlando does give up his poems. We had discussed how bad they are (how bad are they?) and decided that any shortcomings

were in his skill, not his love, and we had compared the two
versions of a Renaissance commonplace in one of his poems and
in *The Tempest*—

> Nature presently distilled
>   Helen's cheek, but not her heart,
> Cleopatra's majesty,
>   Atalanta's better part,
> Sad Lucretia's modesty

and

>   but you, O you,
> So perfect and so peerless, are created
> Of every creature's best!

—quite an instructive exercise in practical criticism.

We found time also to look at pastoral and anti-pastoral
elements, at Jaques and Touchstone, at Orlando's melancholy in
the opening scenes, and at the songs. I would have liked to
spend longer on the ending. I did tell them about Malcolm Evans'
determined demonstration that there are (if my notes are correct)
168 meanings for Hymen's line 'If truth holds true contents' and
that indeterminacy rules, OK, and we did look at the question of
whether mere plot convenience is going on (I used to think so,
now I'm not so sure), and at Jaques' farewell, on which Heather's
comment is interesting:

> The audience are shocked into realising that the man has decided to take action
> against man's faults and that his previous criticism should have been taken
> seriously, not humorously by the characters and the audience. (Made me feel
> guilt.)—A pitiful rather than comical character.

but the whole business needed looking at more closely.

As does much else in what I now find a very interesting play,
delightful and not without significance, *not* a trifle. After much
browsing I found the best criticism of *As You Like It* where I
always thought I would, in James Smith's essay on the play, from
Scrutiny. He treats of seriousness, showing how Rosalind is serious
and Touchstone and Jaques (*pace* Heather) are not. It's arguable
that Smith 'seems to ignore too much of the ordinary playgoer's
response' (Gamini Salgado)—i.e. finding it delightful, but the
necessary adjustments can be made, and he does direct attention
to what the play can show us about what it can be to be serious.
Serious in the understanding of her love shown by Rosalind in
her glad commitment, neither what Caroline called 'humourless,
solemn commitment' (*is* that all we can mean by 'seriousness'?)
nor the blundering of 'brute beasts that have no understanding',
but the glad joy of knowledge, entering upon marriage.

And all over the country the study of literature is diminishing!

As if there were nothing to learn in reflecting on, for instance, the languages of love, in which love makes sense, in which sense may be made of 'the very wrath of love' . . .

Although whether I have persuaded my class of any of this may be doubted.

References

An account of Bill Greenwell's work can be found in his essay in *Sixth Sense*, edited by Antony Adams and Ted Hopkin (Blackie). Carol McMillan is quoted from her *Women, Reason and Nature: Some Philosophical Difficulties With Feminism* (Blackwell, 1982), p. 81. Coleridge's remark may be found in *Shakespearian Criticism*, ed. T. M. Raysor, Vol. 1, p. 121. Philip Edwards' 'The Declaration of Love' is in *Shakespeare's Styles: Essays in Honour of Kenneth Muir*, ed. Edwards, Inga-Stina Ewbank and G. K. Hunter (Cambridge University Press, 1980); John Vyvyan's book is *Shakespeare and Platonic Beauty* (Chatto and Windus). James Smith's essay can be found in his *Shakespearian and other essays* (Cambridge University Press, 1974; would that they would produce a paperback edition of this fine book) and in F. R. Leavis (ed.) *A Selection From 'Scrutiny' Vol. 2* (Cambridge University Press, 1968). Salgado's remark is from *Shakespeare: Select Bibliographical Guides*, ed. Stanley Wells (Oxford University Press, 1973), still a useful collection. On the language of love see Chapters 5 and 6 of Ian Robinson's *The Survival of English* (available from the Brynmill Press); it's also worth pondering some pregnant remarks in an essay by Rush Rhees, 'Religion and Language', in *Without Answers* (Routledge and Kegan Paul, 1969), pp. 121–5. Richard Adams (ed.) *Teaching Shakespeare* (Robert Royce) has a section about students writing as the characters of *As You Like It* looking back on their experience of Arden. Malcolm Evans' post-structuralist reading of the play is in *Signifying Nothing: Truth's True Contents in Shakespeare's Text* (Harvester, 1986); and Terry Eagleton's remarks on the conventions of love poetry are in his *Shakespeare* (Blackwell, 1986). I also made use of C. L. Barber's *Shakespeare's Festive Comedy* (Princeton University Press, 1959) but didn't get round to the other standard works, or to Ruth Nevo's *Comic Transformations in Shakespeare* (Methuen, 1980), which *might* be interesting.

SHAKESPEARE: AN APPROACH TO *HAMLET*

STAFFORD SHERLOCK

C. H. Whitely in an article entitled 'Epistemological Strategies' outlines very neatly the position of the sceptical philosopher who points out that we very often draw incorrect inferences from the visual clues we receive from our experience. 'Smith is yawning', he says, naturally tempts us towards the proposition 'Smith is tired', but there is no logical relationship between these two statements.[1] Smith may equally well be bored or yawning as a reflex action to another person's yawning. What, however, if it can be demonstrated that not only were we wrong about Smith but that we have also been wrong about a whole succession of situations? What happens then is that we plunge into solipsism, and we may regard it as futile in a world of illusions to pursue reality because every phenomenon in merely an appearance. The only possible enduring point of reference is my own frail consciousness.

In the absence of any training in or even introduction to basic philosophical concerns, most of our students will find these ideas difficult, yet if they are to consider *Hamlet* they will need to think about them. Lacking such training students will seize upon the appearance/reality dichotomy and attempt to use it as a key to unlock all the mysteries of the play. Baldly stated, however, this dichotomy is question-begging and, therefore, unhelpful in exploring the complexity of *Hamlet*. Now it is true that at first Hamlet himself seems to have a clear notion of what constitutes reality and what is merely appearance. His irate reply to the Queen's comforting cliché is characteristic of his early state. 'Seems Madam', he retorts, 'Nay it is;'. Here he has no doubts about his ability to distinguish between the two halves of the dichotomy. What he knows 'within' is real; it is clearly distinguishable from 'trappings', 'suits' and 'actions that a man might play'. When, however, Hamlet meets the ghost the effect is ultimately not to sharpen the dichotomy but to destroy it. Initially the ghost does appear to represent reality and Hamlet seizes upon its apparent certainty with eagerness, but this certainty is not a commodity which his 'distracted globe' can keep intact. The dreadful realisation comes that amongst all other appearances this may be another. His mother is only a 'seeming virtuous Queen', Claudius may smile but is still 'a villain' and the ghost itself which comes with all the 'trappings' of certainty 'may be a Devil'. Hamlet then is left floundering in a sea of appearances. In such a world all absolutes disappear; only subjective interpretations of sense-data remain. 'There is nothing good or bad', says Hamlet, 'but thinking makes it so'. There is only one real Cartesian truth, 'Cogito ergo sum'; all else is to be distrusted.

In a customary progression Hamlet the sceptic becomes Hamlet the existentialist as he realises that in the absence of a coherent reality he had better start constructing his own. This is why he must first reject the roles which others would make for him. With my upper sixth group, I paused for some time to discuss Hamlet's conversation with Guildenstern in Act III. It is a section to marvel at. Rosencrantz and Guidenstern are attempting to fulfil two functions for the king; throughout they have been the king's informants but, just as importantly, they have been one of the agencies through which the king has attempted to manipulate Hamlet—to force him into playing a role which is less threatening. Consequently when he hears of Hamlet's interest in the players at the beginning of Act III, he instructs them to 'drive his purpose into these delights'. Hamlet, however, who has been driven by so many forces is attempting now to establish direction for himself. It is a tension which to a lesser or greater extent we all share. Inevitably we began as a group to reflect upon the way we all play the roles to which we are allotted—teacher, student, son, daughter, friend, teenager—and to consider the possibility that each of us is no more than a compilation of the numerous roles we accept or have thrust upon us. Many of my group, however, refused to accept this and wanted to assert that the whole of any individual is much greater than the sum of the various parts which he plays. Hamlet's situation gave us a focus for our discussion. For there is something of the twentieth century sociologist in Guildenstern. He wants to slot Hamlet into a readily identifiable category, to 'sound' his depths, to 'know' what motivates him, to 'pluck out' what makes him essentially different from anyone else. But, in a parabolic action which really does have to be seen as well as read, Hamlet demolishes the assumption upon which Guildenstern bases his strategy. The action of drawing Guildenstern's attention to the recorder is devastating. 'Will you play upon this Pipe?' Hamlet asks ingenuously. It is simply a matter of moving one's fingers and blowing. But Guildenstern cannot even master the complexities of the simplest of instruments 'I have not the skill' he confesses. Hamlet's reply 'S'blood' has the force of a strong expletive. 'Do you think I am easier to be played on than a pipe?' he asks. Can one human being with all his complexity be totally understood and consequently manipulated by another? Polonius's entrance spares us the futility of any response that Guildenstern might have made. The play has many dark patches but there is a degree of triumph in Hamlet's assertion of his own individual 'mystery'. Here he refuses to be directed; 'you cannot play upon me' is a postive affirmation made in the centre of a swamp of uncertainties. Hamlet knows that if he is to survive he must start writing his own script. If the world is only a giant theatre of illustration, then at least one of the plays can be of his creation. Through it he can at least attempt to make sense of his own perceptions, to find a pattern in the apparently inchoate. If he fails to do this, then only real madness remains. Hence the play becomes a dual symbol; it is at one and the same time a metaphor of illusion, and an image of how we attempt to make coherent the chaos which makes up our experience.

There is, of course, nothing new about these ideas but many of our students will find them puzzling. I have found it helpful, therefore, to approach them in a way which is both amusing and thought-provoking. I begin not with *Hamlet* itself but with Tom Stoppard's play *After Magritte*, and with John Berger's account of Magritte's painting called 'The Key of Dreams'. Berger makes the telling point that this painting emphasises that 'the way we see things is affected by what we know or what we believe'.[2] It appears to be a window which is divided into four equal sections. In each section there is a simple representation of a familiar object and underneath each object is an apparent description of it. In at least three of the four representations, however, the words seem to bear no relationship to the object depicted. Hence beneath a white jug is written 'the bird' and beneath the head of a horse is written 'the door'. Furthermore the four objects presented—a jug, a horse's head, a suitcase, and a clock—would appear to have no discernible connection. Students find the painting puzzling and often react to it with incredulity or scepticism. Inevitably, though, they attempt to make sense of it. At first they struggle to find connections between the words and the objects with which they appear to be associated. When this fails they attempt to find some connection between the individual pictures. What is important about this whole exercise is the process which has taken place. Students are forced into a position where they have consciously to attempt to make sense of data which are presented in unaccustomed combinations. Before the next lesson they are invited to continue rocking their preconceptions by trying Gombrich's mirror trick. When we look into a bathroom mirror we see a life-size face. If we then draw a line around the outline of the reflection and step back we are amazed to find that the actual size of the image is no larger than an orange. The principles of geometry tell us to expect this, but our reaction is, nevertheless, always one of 'frank incredulity'.[3]

Gradually the students begin to grasp the difficult concept which is involved here. Reality, it can be argued, is something we make for ourselves. We construct the shapes and patterns which give sense to our experience. This is what we mean by saying that we can or cannot make sense of things. It is not so much a voyage of discovery but an act of construction; even seeing is an active hermeneutic process.

We begin to explore this idea further by reading Tom Stoppard's play *After Magritte* which provides us with an ingenious and hugely enjoyable expression of these issues. For all of the characters in the play the visual clues are the same but each one, in attempting to make sense of what has been seen, offers an interpretation which bears no resemblance to anyone else's. One sees a one-legged footballer hopping through the rain holding a football; another sees an old blind man with a tortoise under his arm. The audience is drawn into the fun as they react to the sets. What are we to make of the opening scene?

> MOTHER is lying on her back on the ironing board, her head to Stage R, her downstage foot up against the flat of the iron. A white bath towel covers her from ankle to chin. Her head and part of her face are concealed in a tight-fitting black rubber bathing cap. A black bowler hat reposes on her stomach. She could be dead; but is not.
>
> THELMA HARRIS is dressed in a full-length ballgown and her hair is expensively 'up'. She looks as though she is ready to go out to a dance, which she is. Her silver shoes, however, are not on her feet: they have been discarded somewhere on the floor. THELMA is discovered on her hands and knees, in profile to the audience, staring at the floor ahead and giving vent to an occasional sniff.
>
> REGINALD HARRIS is standing on the wooden chair. His torso is bare, but underneath his thigh-length green rubber fishing waders he wears his black evening dress trousers. His hands are at his sides. His head is tilted back directly below the lampshade, which hangs a foot or two above him and he is blowing slowly and deliberately up into the recess of the shade.
>
> Gazing at this scene through the window is a uniformed Police Constable (HOLMES). Only his shoulders, his face and his helmet are visible above the sill. He stands absolutely motionless, and might be a cut-out figure; but is not.[4]

What is clear is that whatever I make of it will not be the same as my fellow theatre-goer will make of it. Faced by the zany chaos of Stoppard's sets, each of our brains works frantically to find out some underlying, ordering explanation. Our attempts to do so may be as ludicrous as Foot's, whose construction of the opening scene is contained in these words to Harris.

> I have reason to believe that within the last hour in this room you performed without anaesthetic an illegal operation on a bald nigger minstrel about five-foot-two or Pakistani and that is only the beginning.[5]

Students begin to realise that Stoppard is making them co-creator of the play. The data, as in Magritte's painting, have been presented in such a way that it forces us to search for a pattern of intelligibility where none apparently exists. 'There is nothing good or bad', says Hamlet, 'but thinking makes it so.' Whether the world is a 'goodly frame' or a 'sterile promontory' depends very much upon your point of view. Since reality, if it exists, is unattainable, then the best we can hope for is to find a pattern in our sensations which suggests a degree of coherence to us.

I have found it interesting to approach the play in this way. Students grasp the idea that uncertainty, once created, will not stay outside the walls of our realities, but threatens their very foundations. They begin to see that the simplistic dichotomy between appearance and reality cannot readily be sustained in Hamlet's world. They are quick, also, to relate these ideas to their own experience. This dilemma has for them an immediacy which is not so apparent to those of us who have left adolescence behind. It revealed itself in their willingness to discuss those larger philo-sophical issues which fascinate most of us but would, in the average staffroom be immediate conversation-stoppers. The play gave us opportunities to talk about whether or not we see the world as it is, whether or not we are merely a succession of different states of consciousness, whether or not there is a stable core of being which we can call self, whether or not experience itself has the coherence of a play, whether or not we are really capable of determining our own actions. And, remembering Ophelia as well as Hamlet, we considered the extent to which parents in creating roles for their children run the risk of destroying them. Finally, because many of them were poised at the brink of major changes in their lives, they took the opportunities to air their own excitements and insecurities about physically leaving home, school and neighbourhood and leaving the roles which they play there. Old worlds for them, too, are losing or have lost intelligibility, and they are quick to recognise the pain involved in creating new patterns, in building new worlds when the old have disintegrated into fragments which have to be shored against their ruin. Hamet for all of us then became 'the objective correlative' through which our own worlds were explored.

And, when we moved on to study Eliot's poetry, we became aware of the importance of *Hamlet* to his thought. The shock of meeting in *The Wasteland* the rapid succession of images apparently lacking form or intelligibility was less than it might have been. We were all reminded that when old and trusted edifices collapse then it is difficult to start building again from the 'stony rubbish' which remains.

At the end of the course *Hamlet* once again came to our aid as we began to tackle the narrative complexities of *The French*

Lieutenant's Woman. By the time we had reached chapter thirteen my students had already met and discussed the concepts which Fowles raises there. The position which argues that 'a character is either "real" or "imaginary"' is, he argues, untenable, and can, in its naivety, only be smiled at. 'You do not think of your own past as quite real', asserts Fowles, 'you dress it up, you gild it or blacken it, censor it, tinker with it, fictionalise it in a word, and put it away on a shelf—your book, your romanced autobiography—we are all in flight from the real reality'.[6] Fowles uses the novel, Hamlet uses the play as images of the way in which we daily construct our worlds; both, therefore, return us to the possibility that 'There is nothing good or bad but thinking makes it so'.

Nevertheless, we need not let the sceptics have the last word. Even Fowles implies that there is a 'real' reality from which we fly in constructing our fictionalised versions of it. And, having declaimed that the role of philosopher-king or novelist-god is not for him he does, nevertheless, deftly stick his thumb into the scales as he invites us to weigh up his several conclusions. As we considered the novel together, we all felt that Fowles was not really prepared to grant us complete freedom to make sense of the material as we saw fit. It was apparent to us that for Fowles at least one conclusion had a greater degree of reality than the other; that one shadow in his version of Plato's cave offered a better reflection than the others. For Stoppard, too, there are true and false interpretations of appearance. We do eventually find out that the one-legged, white-bearded footballer was none other than Foot himself with shaving foam on his face. And what of the play which for us generated all these ideas? In *Hamlet*, even though reality seems to be impossibly hidden under innumerable accretions of appearance, we may want to come to the conclusion that it exists after all. The evil which lacks the ontological form it takes in *Macbeth* is not just in Hamlet, for 'something is rotten in the state of Denmark', and, when his own attempts to order experience fail, when his own 'deep plots do pall', when his own play ends in a shambles, then Hamlet suspects that

> There's a divinity that shapes our ends
> Rough hew them how we will

Whether or not this is to succumb to the strongest and most seductive appearance of all was controversial enough to form the basis of a final discussion of this difficult but intriguing play.

References

1. C. H. Whitely, 'Epistemological strategies', Mind, 1969, Vol. 78, pp. 25–27.
2. John Berger, *Ways of Seeing*, Penguin, 1972, p. 8.
3. E. M. Gombrich, *Art and Illusion*, Phaidon Press, 1960, p. 5.

4. Tom Stoppard, *After Magritte*, Faber, 1971, p. 10.
5. Ibid, p. 31.
6. John Fowles, *The French Lieutenant's Woman*, Panther Books, 1977, p. 87.

TEACHING 'WIT, AND POETRY, AND POPE'

PAUL DEAN

Teaching the *Epistle to Dr Arbuthnot* for the J.M.B. 'A' level 'long poem' section, which requires detailed knowledge of the historical background of the chosen text, I became aware how little Pope's work answered to any notion of poetry which my pupils had. Their unconscious neo-Romantic assumptions, which equated the expression of feeling in poetry with its *lyric* expression, prompted them to find Pope 'cold' and 'mechanical'; their media-conditioned notion of Satire as simply destructive disinclined them to search for the corrective norm which underpins all Pope's critical attacks; while their blunted sense of rhythm and movement dulled his infinite variations of the couplet form to a metronomic 'beat'. A glance at past examiners' reports on this part of the syllabus confirmed my suspicion that preparation for this paper could quickly degenerate into cramming, time being too short and the pupils perhaps too reluctant for leisurely exploration. The Report on the 1982 examination, for instance, declared that 'the problem of proving a satisfactory involvement in and understanding of longer period poems remains unsolved by most writers'. Plainly, though, something would have to be done—and this on a text which is exceptionally allusive even for Pope, and on which there is a shortage of good criticism as distinct from exegesis.[1] The emphasis of editors and commentators has seemed to me to fragment the *Epistle*, an approach apparently countenanced by Pope's statement that the poem was 'drawn up by snatches', into a mosaic of set pieces with little to focus or unify it. Accordingly this essay offers, not a commentary on the poem, but some account of how I placed it in its background and dealt with the various problems it posed to the pupils. My approach has since been adapted when presenting other works by Pope or by his fellow-Augustans.

By way of introduction the pupils needed to become attuned to Pope's distinctive 'voice' and procedure, and it happened that they had already studied Chaucer and Donne, so we compared Pope's imitations of these poets with the originals, seeking to establish the changes in the English language and in attitudes towards it which occurred between 1400 and 1700. Johnson, in *Lives of the Poets*, observed that Pope aimed to put Donne into 'smoother numbers'—

the phrase and its assumptions repaid examination (compare a favourite pupil non-comment that the poem 'flows very easily'). Pope's instinct, we found, is to refine and clarify both idiom and rhythm, eliminating the relaxed or the colloquial in the interests of urbanity and perspicuity. In place of the expansive verse paragraphs of his predecessors he works with the couplet, even the single line, as his basic unit, and what in Chaucer is an illusion of easy, vigorous conversation, and in Donne is a 'rough' style suited to the satiric genre, becomes in Pope the lucidly transparent medium of civilised discourse (Chaucer might be discoursing but wasn't 'civilized' in Pope's sense—he wasn't urbane). Classroom analysis and discussion of Pope's alterations, omissions and additions (see Appendix) enabled the pupils to take the force of Johnson's vision in his *Plan of a Dictionary* (1747) that English should be

> laid down, distinct in its minutest subdivisions, and resolved into its elemental principles. And who upon this survey can forbear to wish, that these fundamental atoms of our speech might obtain the firmness and immutability of the primogenial and constituent particles of matter, that they might retain their substance while they alter their appearance, and be varied and compounded, yet not destroyed.

This astonishing anticipation, by one and a half centuries, of Russell's 'philosophy of logical atomism', is worth pondering in connection with Pope's structural habits, and illuminates his apparent tone-deafness to much that is distinctive in Chaucer and Donne. It also leads to consideration of the difference between medieval and Augustan cosmologies, which we might crudely compare to the difference between pictures of the universe as a series of concentric rings and as a series of geological strata. God, Man and Nature are for Chaucer and Shakespeare interdependent: for Pope they are separate, autonomous entities, related by systems of social obligation and logical rather than analogical processes of thought.[2]

The poetry which such a metaphysic produces will aim for maximum clarity and precision of thought and expression, at the expense, if necessary, of richness of texture and multiplicity of meaning—not that Pope lacks these qualities, but we don't apprehend them by reading him as though he were Keats. This is a stumbling-block for many pupils who expect to conduct their explorations of literature through an emotional and sensuous response to metaphor and are oddly unprepared for the demand on their intelligence and wit—a word which, of course, will require a good deal of discussion and illustration in the classroom, leading to consideration of Satire as a genre and to the point that it was the satiric mode which transformed Pope's response to life from a bundle of disparate sensations into a pattern of sensibility.

Pupils will concede that satire is a negative attack, 'knocking', 'taking the mickey', but find its positive aim, in the best writers, puzzling. One reason for this is of course that Pope could appeal to agreed standards and assumptions about human nature which are long gone. Our pluralist and individualist habits of thought recoil from any hint of uniformity ('a kind of dictatorship' one pupil said—rightly in a way). So the *Epistle to Dr Arbuthnot* requires placing in the context of the four Moral Essays which preceded or were contemporary with it in the early 1730s: the *Epistle to Cobham* on the knowledge and characters of men, the *Epistle to a Lady* on the character of women, and the two Epistles to Bathurst and Burlington on the use of riches. In the first two, particularly, we have a more accessible presentation of Pope's theory of human nature than in the *Essay on Man*, which is now all but impenetrable to pupils (and some teachers). As a group the Moral Essays are philosophical, ethical and sociological in their orientation, and the *Epistle to Arbuthnot* extends their concerns to the world of art and the artist's social function, responsibilities and obligations.

A leading feature of these poems is the tension they embody between an awareness that human beings are unique individuals and an impulse to universalise human experience. Subjectivity, irrationality and caprice are acknowledged features of human behaviour (see, e.g. lines 19–24 of the *Epistle to Cobham*), but in themselves they would defeat the kind of poetry Pope wants to write. Accordingly he resorts to a self-contradiction: he declares that, after all, the infinite variousness, *ondoyant et divers*, of humankind is regulated by each individual's Ruling Passion (see lines 174–177 of *Epistle to Cobham*, and lines 206–210 of *Epistle to a Lady*). This enables him to include in the poems both a series of portraits of individuals, seen as types enslaved by various Ruling Passions, and to use their admittedly abnormal behaviour as the basis for generalisations about normal behaviour. The *Epistle to Arbuthnot*, accordingly, explores the Ruling Passions to which artists, especially writers, are prey, and ranges beside the types (Atticus the False Friend, Bufo the Ignorant Patron, Sporus the Court Lackey—further identification of historical personages actually defeats Pope's aim here) the named individuals (Arbuthnot, Pope's parents, Pope himself, or rather his persona in the poem[3]) in whom the Ruling Passion is tempered by a broader humanity.

In the *Epistle to Burlington* Pope addresses the matter of Taste and its relation to Sense (as with Wit, the *OED* entries for these words are worth discussing in class). He makes metaphorical use of the fashion for landscape 'improvement'—an image *we* may apply to his own treatments of Chaucer and Donne and which

Johnson, again, reached for in differentiating Pope from Dryden:

> Dryden's page is a natural field, rising into inequalities, and diversified by the varied exuberance of abundant vegetation; Pope's is a velvet lawn, shaven by the scythe, and levelled by the roller.

Pope advocates a balance, in landscaping, between inspired alteration and cultivation of existing features; beauty is the product of nature plus reason: 'Still follow Sense, of ev'ry Art the Soul,/Parts answ'ring Parts shall slide into a Whole' (ll. 65–66). Timon's villa shows how taste can be misapplied to violate the promptings of reason:

> His Gardens next your admiration call,
> On ev'ry side you look, behold the Wall!
> No pleasing Intricacies intervene,
> No artful wildness to perplex the scene;
> Grove nods at grove, each alley has a brother,
> And half the platform just reflects the other.

> (ll. 113–118)

I used these lines to meet a common pupil misapprehension of Pope's verse, that it is 'artificial' (in our, pejorative, sense: to Pope this would have been a compliment). He distinguishes here between the barrenness which results from treating balance and proportion as ends in themselves, and the successful use of them as means to an end. His own use of these devices in his verse falls emphatically into the second category—it isn't 'aesthetic' in an 1890-ish way, since the engagement of our critical intelligence is assumed. Pope's whole satiric method can, indeed, be thought of as a moral 'improvement', applying sense and reason (i.e., taste) to nature. This, and not dilettantism, is why his verse is minutely landscaped, the formal garden Johnson recognised, rather than the luxuriantly proliferating forest of Chaucer and Shakespeare.

Consideration of the *Moral Essays* thus leads naturally to a summary of the role of the artist in society which Pope will develop in the *Epistle to Arbuthnot*. The world offers a bewilderingly varied spectacle whose apparent chaos menaces our rationality. We are, nonetheless, assured by both reason and revelation that the world is fundamentally ordered, and the artist has a paramount responsibility to demonstrate that providential design by his affirmation of order both thematically and structurally. The satirist, in particular, does this by extolling the true virtues and standards of behaviour which promote individual, social and cosmic harmony, castigating those whose Ruling Passion causes them to deviate from such standards, and showing us that moral 'improvement' is within our grasp.

What seem, then, to pupils to be mere digressions in the *Epistle to Arbuthnot* are in fact 'artful wildness to perplex the scene'. The transitions between Pope's (or his persona's) own life and the wider literary *milieu* point up a telling contrast. On the one hand we have the earnest labour of the young poet, encouraged by eminent men of letters to serve his apprenticeship by working through the standard Kinds, accepting justified criticism meekly and tolerating carping—all this displaying Pope as the embodiment of reason, taste and sense. On the other hand we observe a gallery of lunatics, each possessed by a Ruling Passion for literary fame but devoid of genuine self-knowledge or humility, who besiege Pope for support, demanding advice, letters of introduction, money, even revision of their work. The true artist's responsibility is not to flatter but to dispel their illusions—and this is a *moral* responsibility:

> You think this cruel? Take it for a rule,
> No creature smarts so little as a fool . . .
> Who shames a Scribler? Break one cobweb thro',
> He spins the slight, self-pleasing thread anew;
> Destroy his Fib or Sophistry; in vain,
> The Creature's at his dirty work again!
> Thron'd in the Centre of his thin designs;
> Proud of a vast Extent of flimzy lines.

> (lines 83–84, 89–94)

The bad poet is a parody of God the Creator, a rapacious spider whose constructs ensnare, unlike the good poet who humbly imitates the Divine design. Opposition to bad poets is thus a moral duty because they may mislead their readers into misapprehending nature and the purposes of nature's Creator. Satire, as a weapon against the threatened anarchy, hurts only the intended victim. The same pupils who will enjoy our fashionable media sneerers are, by an unconscious irony, frequently shocked by the virulence of Pope's attack—surely, they exclaim, these people couldn't have deserved *that*? Their liberalism finds it all so *unfair*! But again Pope forestalls their objections in denouncing the man

> Who reads but with a Lust to misapply,
> Make satire a Lampoon, and Fiction, Lye.
> A Lash like mine no honest man shall dread,
> But all such babbling blockheads in his stead.

> (lines 301–304)

to which we should add his prefatory comments to the 'Imitations of Horace':

> And indeed there is not in the world a greater Error, than that which Fools are so apt to fall into, and Knaves with good reason to incourage, the mistaking of a *Satyrist* for a *Libeller*; whereas to a true *Satyrist* nothing is so odious as a *Libeller*, for the same reason as to a man truly *Virtuous* nothing is so hateful as a *Hypocrite*.

Pope's satire is of course personal, but it is also *im*personal in T.

S. Eliot's sense, 'not the expression of personality, but an escape from personality' into something more than *merely* personal.[4] Pope was no saint, and he took his opportunities for settling scores (he had more provocation than many of us). Nonetheless the standards offended against are social, not private to Pope: in denouncing them he is a spokesman as well as an individual. Satire for him is the correction, through purgative laughter, of error, exposed as folly; behind the exposure lies the sense of values shared between writer and reader, so that, far from being coldly aloof as pupils tend to think, his tone is intimate, albeit controlled by decorum.

The *Epistle to Arbuthnot* examines a threatened perversion of cultural ideals which it makes vivid by images of chaos and confusion, most famously in the 'Atticus' portrait with its systematised paradoxes culminating in the brilliantly mimetic couplet 'Now high, now low, now Master up, now Miss,/And he himself one vile Antithesis' (lines 324–325). The functions of critic, patron and courtier are perverted respectively by Atticus, Bufo and Sporus, each an agent of chaos, all trying to drag Pope into their train by attributing their distorting techniques to him:

> The Tale revived, the Lye so oft o'erthrown,
> Th'imputed Trash, and Dulness not his own;
> The Morals blackened when the Writings scape;
> The libel'd Person, and the pictur'd Shape;
> Abuse on all he lov'd, or lov'd him, spread,
> A Friend in exile, or a Father dead.

(lines 350–355)

Once again this is not just self-defence; Pope champions not only his own cause but that of any true artist who strives to maintain the standards necessary to a healthy culture. Parallels are cropping up constantly in our own cultural life, so it is easy to show the pupils that the poem has its continuing point.

Faced with such calumnies the poet flees public life, taking refuge in the trustworthiness of the domestic circle and of private friendships. Hence the praise of Arbuthnot and of Pope's parents, who without any flashily sophisticated pretence exemplify the virtues guaranteeing the order without which society must perish: they 'knew no Schoolman's subtle Art,/No Language but the Language of the Heart' (lines 398–399).

Thus the movement between the public, literary, world and Pope's private life expands in significance until it crystallises an opposition between two systems of value, one based on destructive Ruling Passions and on an anti-Order, the other on self-knowledge and the reflection-by-duplication of order within individuals and works of art. The *Epistle* itself, with its inclusion of both systems and its procedure not of synthesis but of anatomisation, embodies the desired balance. In the revised *Dunciad* Pope was to despair of the victory of order, but at this point in his career he remains hopeful of the effectiveness of the satiric lash, and his poem represents a felicitous match between principle and practice.

When reading pupils' essays on Pope, I have noticed two insidious temptations recurring. One is to suppose that, because Pope paid such attention to the mechanics of his verse, calibrating and re-adjusting until every syllable told, his effects can adequately be discussed in terms of technicalities. Such matters are a lifeline for the intimidated young reader because they seem quantifiable and beyond dispute. Pope, of course, knew this wouldn't do:

> But most by *Numbers* judge a Poet's Song,
> And *smooth* or *rough*, with them, is *right* or *wrong* . . .
> (*Essay on Criticism*, lines 337–338)

—and in the *Epistle to Arbuthnot* he mocks the pedant 'who reads not, and but scans and spells', the 'Word-catcher that lives on syllables' (lines 165–166). Syllables do seem an attractive diet to the young—one pupil claimed that the restriction to twenty syllables per couplet 'makes Pope's comments more sarcastic'. We can see what is being said—the tautness of the chosen medium facilitates the pith and conclusiveness, the epigrammatic bite, at which Pope often aims—but its expression is warping. Arid catalogues of instances of alliteration, assonance, antithesis etc. tell us little or nothing. On the other hand, with Pope more than with many poets there is an impulse to translate—after all, I was told, you said he wrote out prose versions of the poems first, and you told us that we had to look at the content. Again Pope anticipated the problem—he lamented the authors of 'not Poetry, but Prose run mad' who 'my modest Satire bad *translate*' (*Epistle to Arbuthnot*, lines 188–189). So, commenting on

> See skulking *Truth* to her old Cavern fled,
> Mountains of casuistry heap'd o'er her head!
> (*Dunciad*, Book IV, lines 641–642)

another pupil paraphrased: 'Pope is mocking truth, whom he sees as having lost face when her verbal arguments, especially those depending on the ambiguity of a word, were undermined'. Here the direction of the irony is mistaken, and the copying out of some dictionary's definition of 'casuistry' draws attention away from the original. The substitution of the pupil's metaphor, 'undermined', for Pope's, shows a further drift. The progression 'skulking . . . fled . . . heap'd' is completely missed.

It would be uncharitable to take lightly such wrestlings with a poet who is, after all, formidably difficult and now, alas, so remote. What these comments show is that the balance between content

and form, analysis and synthesis, in pupils' reading and writing
about Pope is exceptionally difficult to maintain—and certainly no
easier to maintain in our teaching.

Notes

All quotations from Pope are from the one-volume version of the Twickenham
edition by John Butt, Methuen, 1963. There is a useful school edition of the *Epistle
to Arbuthnot*, together with the *Essay on Man*, by Anthony Trott and Martin
Axford, Macmillan, 1966.

1. One exception is Peter Dixon, *The World of Pope's Satires: an Introduction to
   the Epistles and Imitations of Horace*, Methuen, 1968, pp. 109–121. James
   Sutherland, *A Preface to Eighteenth-Century Poetry*, Oxford, 1948, remains an
   indispensable background book for the teacher.
2. It has been neatly observed that whereas the Elizabethans' dominant fear was
   that things might fall apart, the Augustans' dominant fear was that they might
   merge together (Pat Rogers, *The Augustan Vision*, Weidenfeld, 1974, p. 27).
3. I. R. F. Gordon, *A Preface to Pope*, Longman, 1976, p. 23, stresses the danger
   of taking Pope's persona in the poem for a 'confessional' self-portrait.
4. F. R. Leavis's comment on *The Dunciad* is pertinent here too: 'We don't feel
   the personalities as personal. More than that, we don't, for the most part, even
   in places where animus is very apparent, feel the total effect to be negative,
   expressing a hostile and destructive will' (*The Common Pursuit*, 1952, Peregrine
   ed., 1962, p. 89).

Appendix

I can only give a hint here of the necessary analysis: for instance,
here is the opening of Chaucer's 'Wife of Bath's Prologue':

> Experience, though noon auctoritee
> Were in this world, is right ynogh for mee
> To speke of wo that is in mariage;
> For, lordynges, sith I twelve yeer was of age,
> Thonked be to God that is eterne on lyve,
> Housbondes at chirche dore I have had fyve,—
> If I so ofte myghte have ywedded bee,—
> And alle were worthy men in hir degree.
> But me was toold, certeyn, nat longe agoon is,
> That sith that Crist ne wente nevere but onis
> To weddyng, in the Cane of Galilee,
> That by the same ensample taughte he me
> That I ne sholde wedded be but ones . . . .

Now here is Pope:

> Behond the Woes of Matrimonial Life,
> And hear with Rev'rence an experienc'd Wife!
> To dear-bought Wisdom give the Credit due,
> And think, for once, a Woman tells you true.
> In all these Trials I have born a Part;

I was my self the Scourge that caus'd the Smart;
For, since Fifteen, in triumph have I led
Five Captive Husbands from the Church to Bed.
  Christ saw a Wedding once, the Scripture says,
And saw but one, 'tis thought, in all his Days;
Whence some infer, whose Conscience is too nice,
No pious Christian ought to marry twice . . . .

(lines 1–12)

To point to Pope's constructing in paragraphs and use of capitalised abstractions as evidence of a more apparently logical and generalised handling of the material is simple: more interesting is the difference in tones of voice—Chaucer relaxed, colloquial, unobtrusively engaging, innocently 'reasonable' and ingenuously anxious for enlightenment on the ethics of remarriage; Pope beginning with a 'Behold' indicative of demonstration rather than discourse, and proceeding syntactically with 'hear . . . think . . . for . . . 'tis thought . . . Whence some infer' carrying the reader inescapably from point to point. Chaucer's Wife is an immediately-felt creation with her own speaking voice: Pope's is an eighteenth-century Fair refracted through the superior male mind (notice the 'for once' in Pope's line 4). In Chaucer we are hardly conscious of the couplet medium: in Pope we are hardly conscious of anything else, and the antitheses and alliteration add polish at the expense of Chaucerian vigour. Pope, in short, tidies Chaucer up, and in the process much of what we now consider characteristic of Chaucer has evaporated. There is a sense in which Pope could not read Chaucer—in which he was tone-deaf to Chaucer's distinctive note.

In putting Donne's 'Satyre II' into 'smoother numbers' (as Johnson expressed it) Pope is dealing with a theme nearer to his heart, the relation of individual vice to social corruption. Nonetheless he is still impelled to eliminate disequilibriums of thought and expression. Take this passage where Donne is mocking the Grub-street hacks of his own day:

One, (like a wretch, which at Barre judg'd as dead,
Yet prompts him which stands next, and cannot read,
And saves his life) gives ideot actors meanes
(Starving himselfe) to live by his labor'd sceanes;
As in some Organ, Puppits dance above
And bellows pant below, which them do move.

(lines 11–16)

This becomes in Pope:

Here a lean Bard, whose wit could never give
Himself a dinner, makes an Actor live:
The Thief condemn'd, in law already dead,
So prompts, and saves a Rogue who cannot read.
Thus as the pipes of some carv'd Organ move,
The gilded Puppets dance and mount above,

Heav'd by the breath th'inspiring Bellows blow;
Th'inspiring Bellows lie and pant below.

(lines 13–20)

Donne's contorted syntax and elaborate parenthetical asides disappear as the ideas gain new point from a mind which worked with the single line as the basic unit. The careful balancing of clauses from couplet to couplet (lean Bard against actor: thief against rogue; carved against gilded; heaved up against panting collapse) interposes between us and the poem's 'voice' the filter of the organising intelligence.

JANE AUSTEN: *EMMA*

DAVID HUBAND

I have taught *Emma* twice recently; first to an agreeable and
receptive Sixth Form, and, more recently, to an evening class of
adults. Reflecting on the form of the two courses, the kinds of
lessons we had, and the written work done, it struck me how
different they had been, although my own view of the book had
not substantially altered between teaching the two groups. I suppose that the sort of emphasis which my part in the classes had
given was similar; in both cases I knew I wanted discussions which
grew out of close reading of the text and moved towards some kind
of generalization; and the passages we discussed were largely
identical. Nevertheless, what could be described as the movement
towards the abstraction of pattern and a sense of the wholeness of
the book was much greater with the adult class (which spent about
a quarter of the time the Sixth Form had on the book), not because
of greater literary knowledge or academic expertise but presumably
because of a readiness to respond psychically in a different way.
The point may be an obvious one, but gave me some satisfaction,
since it seemed to reflect that the lessons had taken account of the
way in which we read at different ages, and the fact that Sixth
Formers (or many of them) may be moving from a 'first order'
reading of novels as stories towards a more critical and inter-
pretative reading. Again, I don't claim that the point is original or
not obvious, but it seems to me of the greatest importance that any
'A' level teaching should take account of individual response, and
that the teacher's role is to support and clarify discussion which
stems from a class reading of the text.

The sort of influence which I hoped to have on the lessons can
probably be most clearly seen from the somewhat random reading
which had influenced my own view of the book. I had recently read
Responses to Literature—the Schools Council/NATE report on
examining 'A' level literature—and felt confirmed by this in the
general approach I wished to adopt. Christopher Gillies' *A Preface
to Jane Austen* goes far beyond what a Sixth Former would need to
know, but is good background reading, and has some illuminating
points on *Emma*. In *The Great Tradition*, Leavis has the sentence:

> When we examine the formal perfection of *Emma*, we find that it can be
> appreciated only in terms of the moral preoccupations that characterize the

53

novelist's peculiar interest in life.

which indicated the general direction in which I felt discussion could profitably lead. I had also found deeply interesting Alasdair MacIntyre's *After Virtue*, where he discusses the Aristotelian roots to Jane Austen's view of morality and the 'unity of life' implied by her novels. I certainly felt that if discussion was to move away from the specific 'enactments' of the novel, it could be more usefully steered in the direction of philosophy than of history. Themes which were evident to me in the novel grew, as it were, from the living matter, and I felt little impulse to place it historically or socially. It still seems to me now that this was right, and that discussions of Aristotle and of Utilitarianism that resulted were no bad thing, even though the 'moral preoccupations' to which Leavis refers are specifically to do with *Emma* and can be discussed only in terms of that novel.

These critical books pointed to the areas that I wished to inform our discussion, but the particular episodes on which many of the lessons were initially to be based were chosen as much for their 'dramatic' quality as their being illustrative of any particular theme. I wanted the value of the 'first order' level of reading to be recognized, and was also conscious of a tendency in myself when teaching 'A' level to hold too firmly to a particular interpretation; this in particular when summing up after discussion (mainly so that everyone has something coherent to write down and revise from). This has great appeal to many students, and gives a warm glow to the teacher (it can even pay off in the examination), but I suspect it is inimical to the best kind of critical writing quoted in the report *Responses to Literature*.

I had also found that my own understanding of 'A' level texts had changed considerably over the years, and although it was certainly not the case that one reading was good as another, I had no sense of having reached the ultimate interpretation. The discussion of the text would be the starting point, then, and any summarizing I did would be attempts at a coherent account of the critical points made in class, and would avoid the deathly tidiness of some prescription from on high.

The incidents and conversations which we discussed would, I hoped, shed light on several areas which would be worth discussing. Emma herself, regarded as a quasi-person with a 'psychology', and who develops and matures sufficiently for her to be an eligible marriage partner, was a promising subject, particularly as, in a first order reading, most readers will have a strong sense of her as a person whom, in Jane Austen's words, 'no-one . . . will much like'. From that point, 'psychological' explanations can be constructed, viz: she has been spoiled, has been too much flattered into having an unwarrantedly high opinion of herself, has had so comfortable a life that she seems immune to deep emotional experience, and so on. Thus Emma's attitude to Harriet is explained in terms of a personality nurtured by a given environment. At the same time, her clever, pert answers to Mr. Knightley show her inexperience of the real world, both social and emotional, this being further seen in her relationship with Frank Churchill, development occurring when she recognizes her moral kinship with Mr. Knightley. In other words, a first order reading in terms of 'character', 'relationships', 'development' and so forth, could take us quite a long way.

An essay on 'What kind of man was Mr. Knightley and why did Emma want to marry him?' produced the comment:

> When Mrs Elton calls at Hartfield and refers to him as Knightley, she [i.e. Emma] is furious. 'Never seen him in her life before and calls him Knightley.' I think a tinge of jealously can be detected here. She likes to think of him as a special friend and is a bit put out that Mrs. Elton is so friendly towards him.

This indicates pretty well the way in which the novel was being read; the interpretation 'a tinge of jealousy' comes from the internal dramatic reading by an imaginative pupil. The same essay points out that

> it is not until [her close friendship with Mr. Knightley] is seriously threatened that she realises the real nature of her love for Mr. Knightley [who] shows his love for her by going to console here about Frank's engagement to Jane. This is something that really hurts him as he thinks Emma really loves Frank . . . Both of them display unselfishness by putting the other's well being above their own pain.

This second extract is of a different order from the first, and shows fairly strong teacher/class influence I think. I'm not sure that 'unselfishness' is the pupil's own word, or that it is so close a reading as that implied by 'a tinge of jealousy'. There is, no doubt, a moral element in Emma's readiness for marriage to Mr. Knightley, but the nature of that readiness is clearly seen only by taking account of the strong emotions they both feel. The dichotomy which the essay postulates between the moral and the emotional points to a lack of ease, an unfamiliarity with the second order reading towards which the pupil is moving. The crudeness of the kind of simplification which the statement about Mr. Knightley offers may be inevitable given the stage which the pupil has reached; but it points clearly to the kind of 'education of the feelings' with which reading at this level needs to be concerned. I am aware that the notion of first and second order reading seems to widen the gap that the education of the feelings is attempting to close, and the imprecision of the term is now apparent. It is true that before Emma can marry Mr. Knightley she must 'mature', and that as an adult with a sense of values like his own, she can no doubt be happily married to him; but it is plainly absurd to make this the *sole* reason for his marrying her—that is simply not what the novel is saying. Yet one can see that the tendency in the essay I have quoted is towards that kind of conclusion. Returning to the question which the essay was answering, Emma's realization that Mr. Knightley 'must marry no-one but herself' is not based on an 'unselfish' feeling, but is not for that reason wrong; rather it shows the inadequacy of the concept 'unselfishness' to describe Emma's experience, and indicates the dangers in divorcing second order from first order reading and substituting a moralistic reading for one that is purely imaginative.

Some of the best 'dramatic' readings of *Emma* by the class were of scenes where character is seen in social situations—where a dramatic reading is a valid reconstruction of the novel. I think that only one boy managed to resist *Emma* after these, and that I suspect was a matter of pride. The force of this approach—the sense in which it is 'valid'—results from 'character' manifesting itself in social behaviour; that being so, no social behaviour is 'trivial'. (That *Emma* is in this sense a counter blast to utilitarianism was an argument I used to try and convince the boy, who was still holding out against it, that the novel was 'worthwhile'.) There is a great deal that can come from discussing scenes like Chapter Twelve, where John Knightley presumes to criticise Mr. Perry, the ball at the 'Crown', Mrs. Elton's first conversation with Emma, the Box Hill episode, and so on, where character is realized dramatically and judged in terms of social behaviour. Response to the last of these was one of condemnation, due I think to the effect of the book as a whole. There is in the Box Hill episode a sense of moral crisis, a sense reinforced by the class's understanding of Emma's wish to impress Frank Churchill, her deeper need to please Mr. Knightley and consequent remorse at her failure in the latter. The effect of this is pointed up by Mrs. Elton, and the response of the class to Emma's behaviour was I think partly a recognition of the echoes it has of Mrs. Elton's vulgarity and her husband's behaviour towards Harriet at the 'Crown'. No-one failed to dislike Mrs. Elton, and the class were therefore the readier to feel the full force of Emma's bad manners to Miss Bates. The *cumulative* effect of dramatic readings was important then, in affecting their sense of what counted as bad behaviour. They had by this time absorbed the values of Jane Austen's world; failure to respond to the Box Hill episode could only be by standing outside the book as a piece of creative literature.

The level at which the book was by now being read became evident in a discussion of Mr. Woodhouse. The attitude of the novel towards him is good humoured—the fact that we are amused by his concern for 'young ladies' stockings', for instance, is essential—and moreover insists on respect for him. However, one girl pointed out that her view of Mr. Woodhouse was coloured by the fact that in real life the experience of elderly grandparents living with her was not such a good humoured affair. I think the point was raised because I had said that Jane Austen's view seemed to be that Mr. Woodhouse should be respected for his good qualities, regardless of whether he was irritating or not—a point that seemed born out by her view of what is appropriate to Miss Bates. Certainly there was scepticism in the class about the readiness with which Emma and Mr. Knightley allow Mr. Woodhouse's feelings to weigh so heavily against their marriage. The question here was not so much whether they *would* behave like this, but whether such behaviour would be right. The Box Hill episode presented no such difficulties because everyone could 'feel' Emma's unkindness and the pain it caused Miss Bates. The impulse of the class was clearly to judge behaviour by reference to their own sense of rightness and to discredit the book (one can sympathize with the point of view) where it seems to expect too much.

It is also a difficulty implicit in the kind of approach I had adopted. To see the book in a more historical light could, while attributing social and psychological conditioning to Emma's 'character', avoid judgements made from a personal viewpoint. Clearly *some* historical sense is essential to even first level reading. As one girl wrote: 'There are many examples of observation that are trivial to the modern-day reader, but are not to Jane Austen and the society she writes about.' Quite apart, however, from the value to the pupil of a reading which avoided this kind of judgement, how could we enjoy the awful Mrs. Elton without judging her? In her case, to realize her at all is to judge her; it is part of the reading.

There was general agreement that benevolence of disposition *should* be valued even when there is intellectual inferiority, a view which seems morally irreproachable. I hope this thought made the girl look again at her grandparents, but the notion of what is *owed* where that conflicts with spontaneous feelings not surprisingly created problems not entirely soluble by reasoning.

The other major area we discussed which could take account of the whole span of the novel and which also shed light on the difficulties of judging Emma, was the extent to which she changes during its course. We had already seen Emma displaying the catalogue of deficiencies which any Sixth Form trained in discussion of 'character' can compile, together with some explanation of the given causes for these. The question of her development raises

interesting matter about the influences we see at work on her, and
the significance of the experiences which affect her most. It also
helped to give a fuller account of the importance of marriage, and
in particular of Emma's marriage. It is certainly possible to *feel* the
change in Emma, for instance by comparing the pert knowingness
of her mental rejoinder when Harriet is describing Robert Martin's
mother (p. 58):

> '. . . . Not that she *wanted* him to marry. She was in no hurry at all!'
> 'Well done, Mrs. Martin!' thought Emma. 'You know what you are about.'

with her much later response to Mr. Knightley's praise of her
treatment of Harriet (p. 456):

> 'Much of this, I have no doubt, she may thank you for.'
> 'Me!' cried Emma, shaking her head, 'Ah! poor Harriet!'
> She checked herself, however, and submitted quietly to a little more praise than
> she deserved.

The change was evidently not seen by most of my class as 'drastic'
however. On this topic one pupil wrote:

> Emma clearly does change in many ways. There is never a drastic change though
> and never a point where it can be said to be happening. There is a gradual
> development of character . . . By the end of the novel Emma is a far more
> acceptable character than she was at the beginning although her character then
> should not be completely written off as she showed virtuous qualities then e.g.
> helping the poor and caring for her father.

One does not have to agree totally with this comment to see that
it is in her behaviour that Emma's development is most clearly
seen—the Emma of the earlier parts of the novel is still there,
respecting but not totally submitting to Mr. Knightley, and this
continuity in her character is evidently perceived in the essay. The
sort of account that I think the essay is moving towards is that a
measure of Emma's maturity will be her ability to see the connection between her behaviour towards her father and her behaviour towards Miss Bates. One can see again the crudeness of the
description, and its inadequacy to convey the subtlety of what the
novel gives us, in 'virtuous qualities'; it is 'virtuous' in Emma to
respect her father, but there is also family pride—she is unwilling
to admit his inadequacies because this would reflect on herself.
When Emma insults Miss Bates it is not *simply* her lack of virtue
but her response to Frank Churchill which caused it; or perhaps
one should say her susceptibility to his flattery causes a suspension
of her virtue. This was picked up in the same essay when the writer
says:

> Her behaviour at Box Hill showed frustration and this may have been because
> of her relationship with Frank as it was superficial and Emma was in need of
> something deeper.

The difficulties for this writer are again evident; how to convey the psychical immaturity which is a part of Emma's morally bad behaviour. The discussion has now moved through the kinds of experience which Jane Austen sees as significant for Emma's development—in particular the remorse which she feels after Mr. Knightley's rebuke at Box Hill—to how important it is that her feelings should be touched deeply by life before she can feel deeply enough to want to marry.

The problem for the student at this stage is to grasp the totality of the experience—to see how feelings are a part of moral choices made. One can see in the passage quoted above how the writer views Emma's behaviour at Box Hill in terms of the feelings aroused in her by Frank Churchill (a 'psychological' explanation); but Emma's behaviour is seen earlier in this essay as being 'rude to Miss Bates'. The interpretation by the student rests, then, on psychology and manners. In what sense, one might ask, can Emma's treatment of Miss Bates be considered morally significant? In this pupil's writing, the account is restricted to either one explanation (the psychological) or the other (the moral), while what the novel gives us is a total action which subsumes both— and the writer's failure to perceive *that* indicated pretty clearly the direction which her literary education needed to take.

I have dwelt on this aspect of teaching *Emma* in part because it seems to me that the nature of the book demands discussion of this kind; it is, as Leavis says, inescapably a moral book, taking 'moral' to mean something both subtler and more particular than following a code. I would stress that the *text* was always of primary importance in the discussions we had, both as a starting point and as far as was possible as a final authority, but the degree of teacher direction in discussion must also be evident in the account I have given of the lessons we had. The fuller answer, for example, to the question of Emma's attitude to her father, as I have implied above, depends on an understanding of Emma's maturity in making the connection between the values internal to family life and those pertaining to the wider society in which as an adult Emma must take her place, but to perceive that makes particular demands on the maturity of perception of the reader. My own role was in helping the class to see what is the peculiar value of *Emma*, that it is a book about someone in a situation much closer to that of Sixth Form students than they realize at a first reading.

References

1. John Dixon and John Brown, *Responses to Literature: what is being assessed?* Schools Council Publications, 1985.
2. Christopher Gillie, *A Preface to Jane Austen*, Longman, 1985.
3. F. R. Leavis, *The Great Tradition*, Penguin, 1966.

4. Alasdair Macintyre, *After Virtue: a study in moral theory*, Duckworth, 1981.
5. Page references to *Emma* are to the Penguin edition.

GERARD MANLEY HOPKINS

SUE HILLS

Earnest, earthless, equal, attuneable, vaulty, voluminous, . . . stupendous
Evening strains to be time's vast, womb-of-all, home-of-all, hearse-of all night.[1]

'Granted that it needs study and is obscure.'[2] These words, used by Hopkins himself in relation to 'The Wreck of the Deutschland', might easily be applied to the majority of his poems—not least to the section from 'Spelt from Sibyl's Leaves', quoted above. The subject, the attenuating 'evening', coming six adjectives after the opening of the poem, could be lost to the new reader who, unfamiliar with the stress thus attached to 'evening', would see little but a list of seemingly random words. It is the apparent obscurity of Hopkins' writings which is the initial problem for 'A' level students.

It is also this obscurity, however, which can inspire an immediate fascination: here is one of our 'lesser great poets' (or 'great lesser poets') and we don't understand what he is trying to communicate or why he has chosen to adopt such an alienating approach . . . .

It was this hunger to understand that I used as a way in to a study of his work. A novice in relation to a reading of Hopkins myself, I studied alongside my students in the attempt to come to terms with what he had to say.

His verse, he repeatedly tells us, is 'for the ear' not 'the eye' and thus it seemed appropriate that from the beginning we focussed on the spoken effect of his poetry. Initially, I had no choice but to ignore the manner in which the verse was intended to be read; I had to rely on the students' intuitive ability to register the stressed, the unstressed and the general movement of each piece. All the members of the group were asked to prepare a reading of any Hopkins' poem and to give an extended 'catalogue of thoughts' on that choice. Since this work was designed to culminate in a type of performance in which each of the students was required to take part, I knew that they would be forced to read a number of poems for themselves and I worked on the assumption that most of them would sift through the text to find poems they could understand. And this is indeed what happened. One of the first poems we looked at in this 'glancing' manner was a poem called 'Brothers'. Interestingly, very few of the Hopkins' poems are directly about people. It was significant but perhaps not surprising that this poem should have been the starting point. 'Brothers' is a simple account

61

of how moved the writer was by the love of a boy for his brother:
'the subject of the poem is the vicarious anxiety which the boy
Henry suffers as he watches his brother John act in a play. John
was 'brass-bold' and Henry need not have feared for him. That he
did feel and indeed wholly identify himself with his brother is what
moves Hopkins almost to tears.

> Ah, Nature, framed in fault,
> There's comfort then, there's salt.
> Nature, bad, base and blind
> Dearly thou canst be kind
> There dearly then, darly
> I'll cry thou canst be kind.

It is the grace of such a natural expression of love that moves
Hopkins so deeply. There is nothing sentimental about the poem;
Nature is seen as 'base' and 'bad'. What is remarkable, Hopkins is
saying, is that out of baseness and evil such sweetness and selfless-
ness can spring. 'Brothers' is in fact, a very fine expression of
Hopkins' attitude to nature and to all things in the natural world.'[3]

This 'graciousness of natural love' was something that a mature
second year 'A' level group was capable of responding to and I
was thankful, as I was to be throughout the work on this poet, that
we had not begun a close study of his writing the previous year.
The real advantage of a brief discussion of a poem such as
'Brothers'—apart from defining what was to become one of the
major themes we discussed: the quest for selflessness—was that
the students gained confidence precisely because the poem was
immediately accessible. All I had done was to ask the pupil who I
knew would choose this type of poem to read and comment first.
I then selected other readers equally carefully, using what I knew
about them as people to develop the direction of the sessions. This
gentle introduction to Hopkins finished with an examination of
'Moonrise':

> I awoke in the midsummer not-to-call night, in the white and the walk of the
> morning:
> The moon, dwindled and thinned to the fringe of a fingernail held to candle . . . .[4]

The choice of this particularly beautiful section of poetry, demon-
strating clearly what Hopkins had learnt from 'cynghanedd',[5] and
the student's delight with the image of the moon, enabled us to
focus on two aspects of Hopkins' writing which were to become
increasingly significant—the strikingly apt almost metaphysical use
of imagery and the lilt of the language achieved through internal
half-rhyme. Convinced, as I was not, that 'Moonrise' was merely
a description and unaware of the complexities of Hopkins' attempt
to inscape language in order to re-create the poignancy of the
moment, the student argued that she just liked the sound of the

words. Hopkins writes:

> For indeed I was not over-desirous that the meaning of all should be quite clear, at least unmistakable, you might, without the effort that to make it all out would seem to have required, have nevertheless read it so that lines and stanzas should be left in the memory and superficial impressions deepened, and have liked some without exhausting all. I am sure I have read and enjoyed pages of poetry that way. Why, sometimes one enjoys and admires the very lines one cannot understand.[6]

We were to keep coming back to this statement: partly for reassurance; partly because we discovered this was the only way to begin an appreciation of Hopkins.

The next stage was to look more closely at the themes which were emerging even from a superficial study of his work. I chose to read 'The Wreck of the Deutschland' for this purpose. On reflection, this was probably a mistake. 'The Wreck' is notoriously difficult and very long, running to thirty-four eight line stanzas. I made the choice because the poem looks forward to and in a sense embraces, the themes to be found in the rest of the poems. The other important aspect of 'The Wreck' is the paradox the poem reveals—the paradox apparent even in the first stanzas and 'neatly' resolved by the end:

> The frown of his face
> Before me, the hurtle of hell
> Behind, where, where was a, where was a place.
>   I whirled out wings that spell
> And fled with a fling of the heart to the heart of the Host
> My heart, but you were dove-winged, I can tell.
>   Carrier-witted, I am bold to boast,
> To flash from the flame to the flame then, tower
>   from the grace to the grace.[7]

The problem of the two seemingly irreconcilable opposites—the God who is the fierce taskmaster of all and the God who is the God of 'grace' and 'forgiveness'—is the paradox which asserts itself again and again, finding full expression in 'The Terrible Sonnets' (which I suggest should be read last and critically appraised with the teacher leading the discussion carefully). It is useful to locate the emergence of the paradox in a reading of Hopkins as early in the course as possible.

I began the investigation of 'The Wreck of the Deutschland' by reading copies made of an article 'The Loss of the Deutschland' which appeared in *The Times* on Saturday 11th December 1875. It was this article which inspired Hopkins to write his first poem.

> When in the winter of '75 the Deutschland was wrecked in the mouth of the Thames and five Franciscan nuns, exiles from Germany by the Falck laws, aboard of her were drowned I was affected by the account and happening to say so to my rector he said that he wished someone would write a poem on the subject.

> On this hint I set to work and though my hand was out at first, produced one.
> I had long had haunting my ear the echo of a new rhythm which now I realised
> on paper . . . .[8]

What comes out of the poem is not simply a dedication to the heroic stance of the nuns but an unconventional way of writing realised not just in the innovatory set of techniques but as a consequence of the poet's own conflicting thoughts: the 'new rhythm', endemic to the poem, itself mirrors the pull and tussle of the poet's principles at odds with each other—the struggle Hopkins was to confront time and time again.

It was in the close study of this poem that we first discovered the terms which become so familiar to any student of Hopkins—the terms he coined: 'inscape' and 'instress'. It is not the purpose of this article to try and define these terms but it is important that the teacher attempts a means of explanation for the benefit of the pupils. In my attempt to do so I moved away from the text but not before we had read an extract from 'On the Origin of Beauty—A Platonic Dialogue'. In this piece a Professor of Aesthetics and a student discuss the possibility of defining 'Beauty'. Only one third of the essay is published in the edition we used but even within this section Hopkins comes close to expressing his theory of individualism through the ideas of the Professor:

> The picture that had only one mass put in was unbeautiful: now as it was to be beautiful when both masses were put in, we might suppose that beauty must lie all in that mass which was yet to come: when however we in our second picture, anxious to have our beauty as soon as possible, put the second mass in first, pregnant as it was with graces, lo and behold! the result was as uninteresting as when we had the first mass alone put in. What are we to say then? The beauty does not lie in this mass or in that but in what? In this mass supported by that, and in that as supported by this. Is it so?'
> 'Exactly.'
> 'And artists call this composition. Does not then the beauty lie in the relation between the masses?'[9]

Reading the poem 'Pied Beauty' alongside this section clarified the discussion for the students who found this introduction to the world of aesthetics difficult to comprehend.

> Glory be to God for dappled things—
> For skies of couple-colour as a brinded cow;

I then set a number of specific questions on the Platonic Dialogue which demanded fully worked through written answers in order to help the students forge links between a definition of Beauty and Hopkins' attempts to recreate the experience of 'Beauty' by 'inscaping' language.

I explained my personal understanding of 'inscape' as simply as possible. I began with the experience common to many—and it is difficult here not to resort to cliché—of a snatched moment of creative calm—a point where all the senses and emotions are held and the individual finds him/herself 'instressed' as it were—affected by an elemental force which Hopkins saw as God—and becomes as a result, in tune with earth's natural energies. I saw it as a point where an aspect of beauty in a contrasting environment and the mood of the individual cohere—the one affected by and balanced by the other. I used Eliot's place 'where all the waters meet'; Virginia Woolf's 'Moments of Being' and Keats' 'Negative Capability' to amplify my thoughts, realising that as I spoke of them and gave examples, I was ignoring their complexities. All these, however, I saw as having some bearing on what Hopkins wanted us to recognise when we tried to understand his 'thisness' or 'the essential essence' of for example 'a single snowdrop'.

The students were asked to consider whether or not they had undergone such an experience—and if so, to share it with the group if possible. The one person who was hesitant in accepting this challenge, feeling it was an intrusive act, did, in fact, contribute and interestingly his revelation was by far the most poignant. All the incidents related were set against backgrounds of 'especial' beauty and perhaps half of the group came close to understanding that whatever had moved them into this momentary state of harmony had a particular significance of its own as distinct from other aspects of the experiences they described. Trying to move them further towards an understanding of Hopkins' attempt to inscape language, I suggested they brought in works of art which had affected them in such a manner. The group was much less willing to be drawn here, so I arranged for them to bring in their poems, their music, their paintings on a day when I knew I would not be there. I discovered later that many of them had managed to talk to each other of their responses without having to cope with the presence of a 'critical audience'. I knew why I had to step back but it saddened me and reminded me of what my Head of Department was often saying—that one of the main difficulties in teaching literature to sixth formers was that they had not been 'educated' to talk about feeling without acute embarrassment.

As equipped as they were likely to be to handle Hopkins' intense response to Beauty, we looked closely at several poems, approaching each session as a lesson in practical criticism but making the necessary links between one poem and another. I took each poem in the order found in Gardner's edition[10] with the exception of 'Binsey Poplars'. This we studied first because the techniques the students had to grasp are easy to locate in that poem and it is clear how the finely contrived use of Sprung Rhythm matches the meaning: we hear the swing of the axe as its blade

butchers the trees even as we read. Fortunately, it is not possible
to discuss rhythm, compression, alliteration, omission, half-rhyme
or repetition as a mere clinical exercise when examining Hopkins'
work: techniques and theme are so clearly interwoven. I kept the
explanation of Sprung Rhythm to a minimum—believing that all
the students needed to understand was that Hopkins' innovation
(which he declared had been used by Milton anyway) just consisted
(in his words) 'of scanning by accents or stresses alone without any
account of the number of syllables so that a foot may be one long
syllable or it may be many light and strong'.[11] We kept in mind
the poet's motives—'Sprung Rhythm makes verse more stressy', it
gives the poet a 'flexibility' and it comes closer 'to the rhythms of
speech and prose'. I did have to give a short lecture on metre. I
don't lecture as a rule but here it was necessary since a discussion
on the unconventional would have made little sense without knowledge of the conventional. Happily, teaching of poetry in the lower
school—if it takes place at all—does not include an appreciation
of 'iambic pentameter' and my students did not find the business
of metre difficult. It helps if the teacher adopts a light hearted
approach and laces the session with amusing examples.

I selected about twelve poems which we approached as a class
and which we analysed in detail. I prepared the poems carefully
although I did not use many critical texts. I did read a lot but I
didn't find much that was particularly helpful. Often I found I just
wanted a text to tell me what a specific line meant but writers of
such texts probably found paraphrase as impossible as anyone else.
The most useful book I used and quite sufficient as a starting point,
covering most of what is needed at 'A' level was one of the Preface
Series: Graham Storey's *A Preface to Hopkins*.[12] I would also
recommend Margaret Bottrall's[13] compilation of critical essays in
the Casebook Series. I don't encourage students to use critical
texts and I didn't in the teaching of Hopkins. Using critics' work
has to be a creative process and there are few 'A' level students
who can handle this successfully. The poems which needed a
closer study than any critical text encouraged I worked at through
discussion with my colleagues and students. Those I selected for
close analysis were: 'The Wreck of the Deutschland', 'The Wind-
hover', 'Binsey Poplars', 'Duns' Scotus' Oxford', 'Harry Ploughman', 'Henry Purcell', 'Spelt from Sibyl's Leaves', 'The Terrible
Sonnets'. The students were expected to write on at least three of
these. Other significant poems such as 'To What Serves Mortal
Beauty?', 'The Starlight Night' . . . I allocated to each member of
the group—sixteen in all. The students were given two weeks to
come to terms with their given poem. I allocated each poem with
some thought, giving the most difficult to those whom I knew could

cope with them. I gave specific guidelines to help them work out their reports. For example themes had to be located and linked to other poems; at least two images had to be explained; the effect of technique and form had to be referred to. Then the students met and discussed their readings without direction or interference from me. By this point I was running out of time and rather than comment on each contribution, I added to and qualified their written criticisms; asked for them to be typed by the Resources Department and made up individual bookets for each of the students to keep.

The group wrote their own notes on the prose section and we read the letters when they were appropriate to the reading of a particular poem or the discussion of a specific technique. I also prepared a sheet which directed them towards what I believed to be the important aspects of the letters.

'A' level students should work on their own occasionally and once a couple of prose sections had been studied together I thought the writing from 'Notebooks and Journals'[14] was suitable material for individual work.

In the last sessions on Hopkins we drew our findings together. We discussed Hopkins as an innovator, as a scientist, as a religious poet; we discussed his delight in detail, his attitude to nature, his concern for the neglect and destruction of the environment, his intense regard for beauty, his obscurity and the nature of the spiritual crises he undergoes, apparently resolved by the end of his life. The background work had been done throughout the weeks of study and the step that had to be taken to make some sort of sense of the whole text was not as difficult as I had anticipated it would be.

Perhaps because I was unsure of my ground I insisted that at least five essays were written. In fact I was so concerned that my faltering attempts to help my pupils come to terms with the verse had left them feeling insecure that I invited outside speakers to lead general sessions. One was a colleague who had read a considerable amount of Hopkins and the other was a poet in her own right who had a special regard for his work. The former talked about Hopkins the priest and poet; the latter took the group through how certain poems worked. These lectures were welcomed by the students and made them feel they were 'about something important!' I would certainly repeat the exercise but perhaps for a more laudable reason than the one outlined above. I also invited a Jesuit Priest to take part as I felt the students were receiving uninformed comments on the religious context of Hopkins' poems but he wanted to know how much he was to be paid for each session. So much for educating the public in the ways of the Lord!

I did not find a lack of religious conviction a problem although I had to work hard at the biblical references. The problem I found was having to admit that there were sections of the poems I could not understand. However, I believe that because, on occasions, I was prepared to express my inability to comprehend, we struggled as a whole group to come to terms with the intellect of this poet and gained much as a result of the 'collective enterprise'. The students had to rely on an impressionistic response to parts of the verse and perhaps, in the end, they learned more about the way poetry really works.

References

1. Gerard Manley Hopkins: 'Spelt from Sibyl's Leaves' in *Poems and Prose*: Selected and edited by W. H. Gardner, (Penguin edition, 1975).
2. 'Letter to Bridges', May 13th, 1878, in Gardner, op. cit.
3. Elizabeth Jennings: *The Unity of Incarnation*: Casebook on G. M. Hopkins, edited by Margaret Bottrall, p. 199, 1975.
4. G. M. Hopkins: 'Moonrise' in Gardner, op. cit.
5. Gardner, op. cit.
   Editor's Notes: Additional Notes on the prose, Note B and C.
6. 'Letter to Bridges', op. cit.
7. G. M. Hopkins: 'The Wreck of the Deutschland' in Gardner, op. cit.
8. 'Letter to Dixon', October 5th, 1878, in Gardner, op. cit.
9. G. M. Hopkins: 'On the Origin of Beauty—A Platonic Dialogue' in Gardner, op. cit.
10. Gardner, op. cit. Examination Text.
11. 'Letter to Dixon', op. cit.
12. G. Storey: *A Preface to Hopkins*. Preface Books (Longman), 1981.
13. *Gerard Manley Hopkins*: A Selection of Critical Essays. Edited by Margaret Bottrall (Macmillan), 1975.
14. Gardner, op. cit.

THE POETRY OF EDWARD THOMAS:
a matter of tone

IAN BRINTON

When I have come across the poetry of Edward Thomas on an 'A' Level examination syllabus the text invariably referred to has been the Faber selection of poems edited by R. S. Thomas. This was compiled before much close critical analysis, including dating of the poems, had been completed. More recently however there has been the opportunity of using *The Collected Poems*. Published as an Oxford paperback it not only places the poems chronologically but also presents notes which are both academic and sparing. The inclusion of Thomas's 'War Diary' as an appendix to the volume is a bonus.

Before embarking on the poetry which I was to teach to ten second-year sixth boys I was aware of two major difficulties. Firstly, odd though this may sound, was the difficulty of reference. These boys in the heart of the industrial north did not know what a sedge-warbler looked or sounded like. They were unaware of the difference between the clarity of a thrush's song and the imitative chattering of a starling. On the simplest level they were unaware of the look of nettles dust-covered in the corner of a farmyard, making it difficult for them to register the associations which the poet made cling about so seemingly ordinary a moment. And then swifts, celandines, charlock, tench and combe? Much of Thomas's verse is placed in a specific rural landscape and any dictionary definition of an unknown word would not yield the sort of under-standing needed to engage with the shy and delicate tone. Thomas's poems are often composed of unobtrusive moments residing on the edge of consciousness and, in marked contrast with the poetry of T. S. Eliot where a handbook of references can take one a long way in terms of elucidation, their tone is subtly resistant to analysis. As F. R. Leavis wrote in *New Bearings in English Poetry*, a passage to which I shall return later:

> Thomas is concerned with the finer texture of living, the here and now, the ordinary moments, in which for him the 'meaning' (if any) resides.

In addition to these problems I was aware that since so much of Thomas's verse is engaged with the personal there would be a need at some point to introduce a certain amount of biographical

information. I certainly had no intention of delivering introductory
lessons of potted history because I wanted the boys to experience
the poetry first; but out of close textual analysis questions would
be raised that could be excellently answered by a selective reading
list. Primarily I sent them to Helen Thomas's charming and moving
account of their life together, *As It Was* and *World Without End*.
In addition I pointed to John Moore's *Life and Letters*, William
Cooke's *Critical Biography* and Eleanor Farjeon's *Edward
Thomas, the last four years*. Unfortunately the excellent *Portrait*
by Professor R. G. Thomas had not at this time been published. I
would in future send pupils to that volume without hesitation. I
think that in the case of Edward Thomas it is useful to know
something of the financial pressures upon him, the desperate house-
moving (ten times in seventeen years), the obsessive walking and
note-taking.

I decided to begin the poetry by looking at the early and very
fine 'Old Man'. Here I knew we would be faced by many typical
aspects of Thomas's poetry: the contemplation of past and future,
the importance of memory, the stylistic devices of conversational
reflection and wry irony. I wanted 'Old Man' to act as an introduction to the Thomas world and therefore did not want to go into
the realms of comparing the poem with the earlier prose draft held
in the Lockwood Memorial Library: that sort of critical concern
could wait until much later when we contemplated the effects of
Robert Frost upon Thomas the prose writer. Initially I read the
poem twice aloud to the group and then asked them to think about
the type of experience which was being evoked. One boy's reaction
was that Thomas's feeling seemed akin to that which one has upon
waking out of a dream: we remember the essence, such as absolute
happiness, but cannot recall the action which was the reason for
the happiness. Needless to say I was delighted by the response and
we went on to discuss the particular nature of the herb, old man,
the scent of which acts as a stimulus for the poet's memory: the
bitter distinctive aroma is a potential key to the past. It was at this
point that one boy suddenly exclaimed at the oddity of the names
in the first line: 'Old Man, or Lad's Love'. The contradiction in
the name suggested a key to the future as well as to the past and
contained a delicately balanced sense of loss when placed the other
way round in the second line:

> Old Man, or Lad's Love,—in the name there's nothing
> To one that knows not Lad's Love, or Old Man.

From here we looked at the way in which Thomas registers an
increasing sense of loss and bewilderment as the poem progresses
and found ourselves dwelling upon the personal voice evoked so

sensitively in the third verse:

> As for myself
> Where first I met the bitter scent is lost.
> I, too, often shrivel the grey shreds,
> Sniff them and think and sniff again and try
> Once more to think what it is I am remembering,
> Always in vain.

These lines demand to be read aloud: the repetition, the carrying over of emphasis between lines four and five, the downward movement towards the phrase 'in vain'. It was at this point that I introduced the Berg Notebook entry of 11 November 1914:

> Old Man scent, I smell again and again not really liking it but venerating it because it holds the secret of something of very long ago which I feel it may someday recall, but I have got no idea what

and as the end of the forty-minute lesson approached I read them the few lines concerning the *Key of Knowledge* volume which Thomas had received as a school-prize and the loss of which haunted him down the years until he recorded it in the unfinished autobiography:

> The words, 'The Key of Knowledge', occurred in its title or they stood out somewhere else. It was illustrated by coloured pictures. But it disappeared, I have never had any idea how, before I had read far into it, and I never saw it again. From time to time down to the present day I have recalled the loss, and tried to recover first of all the book, later on the thread of its story, something that would dissipate from its charm the utter darkness of mystery.

From the beginning we were embedded in the Thomas mindscape, the distinctive features of which are a desire to retrace paths to bring past experience alive and the gazed-upon impossibility of doing this: a present moment, sharply perceived, informed by a sense of the past irretrievably lost but haunting in its echoes.

Because of the way in which the opening discussion had gone I decided to pursue the theme of Thomas's restless searching for an untraceable past, an Eden-like quality of experience embodied in the English countryside, the compulsive seeking of the nympholept. So, after 'Old Man' we looked in turn at 'Over the Hills' and 'Lob'. In the former we examined the maze-like meandering of a mind trying to re-enter another world. One pupil wrote:

> The powerful images of the past struggle to manifest themselves in the present for Thomas. A paradox is created in the lines 'I did not know my loss/Till one day '. . ./I leaned upon my spade and saw it all': Thomas's spontaneous but dim perception of that moment and experience reveals to him his sense of loss. His perception lies 'far beyond the sky-line', within the reality of his mind, not the reality of an objective visualised scene . . . The images of the 'restless brook', 'the waterfall' and 'the lake that rests and stirs not in its nook' do seem to represent the psychological motifs of the birth experience and metaphorically the relationship between man and time.

Clumsy though some of this is (what can an 'objective visualised scene' look like?) I was delighted by the urgency of response and we moved quickly on to the long poem 'Lob'. Here we faced immediate problems: the references to particular wild flowers, to country customs and cherished folk-lore seemed a world away from central Leeds. They responded quickly to the opening verse, seeing a link between a world which seems to be so clear and yet disappears when looked for more actively:

> They thought as there was something to find there,
> But couldn't find it, by digging, anywhere.

It was at this point that I quoted the passage from Leavis's *New Bearings:*

> It is as if he were trying to catch some shy intuition on the edge of consciousness that would disappear if looked at directly.

From here the group registered the confusion and pathos of the opening of the second verse where Thomas cannot look directly at an experience since it tends to vanish:

> To turn back then and seek him, where was the use?
> There were three Manningfords—Abbots, Bohun, and Bruce:
> And whether Alton, not Manningford, it was
> My memory could not decide. . . .

They found, on the whole, the remainder of the poem less satisfying on account of its detail and so rather than pursuing at the moment what was for them an alien world we turned to the more visual and metaphorical 'The Path' where the 'legendary/Or fancied place', by being less defined, was more accessible on their own terms.

Since the boys were so taken with this vain attempt at recall and the desire to turn back and re-find oneself I decided to query their response. Was Edward Thomas being sentimental? Was he doing much more than regretting a past world? I am glad to say that they reacted angrily and accused me of being insensitive. After all, as one pointed out, sentimentality associates itself with consciously cultivated emotions whereas Thomas's poetry gave one a personal voice which, albeit reflective and wistful, was honest in tone. Another boy pointed out that sentimentality is also associated with vagueness whereas Thomas's poetry is located firmly in a shared landscape of particularities. So the next obvious step was to look at those poems where Thomas reveals his awareness of what could be poisonous in the search for the past, notably 'Sedge-Warblers' and 'Home 2'. We examined in detail the opening lines of 'Sedge-Warblers' noting the association of 'beauty' and 'dream' and the time 'Long past and irrecoverable'. The particular landscape of yellow buttercup and kingcup jarred when one evaluated the word 'brass' and 'nourishing' became double-edged as the river bore a mythical feminine figure on its surface: a merging of mystical sterile stasis and the countryside so beloved of the poet. The form delighted in the way that Thomas recognised the narcotic effect of the opening lines and turned his back upon that dream, whilst at the same time they admired the truth and skill of the artist who could capture verbally such a visual metamorphosis:

> And yet rid of this dream, ere I had drained
> Its poison, quieted was my desire
> So that I only looked into the water
> And hearkened, while it combed the dark-green hair
> And shook the millions of the blossoms white
> Of water crowfoot . . .

The 'hair' remains from the narcissistic vision and 'shook', with its association with tresses, keeps so faintly in mind the merging of dream into reality of water crowfoot. The ending of the poem with the sedge-warblers whose song 'lacks all words, all melody,/All sweetness almost' was seen as an achievement of reality and an appreciation of an immediate world at the expense of nympholeptic indulgence. I had deliberately introduced the world 'nympholepsy' because it seemed to apply itself so appropriately to this aspect of Thomas's poetry and I placed it in context in the next lesson by taking in copies of Swinburne's 'A Nympholept':

> An earth-born dreamer, constrained by the bonds of
>   birth

Some of the group were quite shocked at the eloquent vagueness of the long poem and dissatisfied with the poeticising which Swinburne indulges in and so I presented them also with D. G. Rossetti's sequence of four sonnets, 'Willow-Wood'. These, accompanied by some Pre-Raphaelite paintings, served as a judicious reminder of Thomas's firm grasp upon the here and now and to endorse the comparison we next looked at 'Home 2'. Here the blurring of individuality is presented in terms of a man immersed in nature:

> 'Twas home; one nationality
> We had, I and the birds that sang,
> One memory.

The lack of distinction here between man and nature, akin to a narcotic selflessness or passivity, is replaced firstly by the song of one bird and then more firmly by the accurate description in the last verse, ending on a note equivalent to the song of the sedge-warblers:

> The sound of sawing rounded all
> That silence said.

The accumulation of small details, the unobtrusive signs, in these poems acted as a bridge to our next concern: those short poems, 'Tall Nettles', 'Adlestrop', 'The Pond', where simplicity is almost deceptive in that one notes the presence of the moment and yet wonders what is the emotional resonance, what Leavis called 'the inner theatre'. Of 'Adlestrop' one boy noted:

> The poet looks around at the stillness of 'willow, willow-herb and grass' as 'still and lonely fair' as the clouds and as he does so the one moment of a blackbird singing is expanded in the silence to a moment in which he hears, 'farther and farther off' the singing of all 'the birds of Oxfordshire and Gloucestershire': the 's' and 'sh' sounds recreating the sensation musically.

Yet again, despite the clumsiness of some of the expression, it seemed to me that the group were stumbling towards the recognition of a very fine sense of tone. How to communicate that recognition to 'A' Level examiners was mercifully still some months away.

In order to pursue this notion of emotional value being placed in a particularised landscape I brought in two short modern American pieces, 'Marin-an' by Gary Snyder and 'Lying in a Hammock at William Duffy's Farm in Pine Island, Minnesota' by James Wright. The first of these opens with a series of details relating to time and space:

> sun breaks over the eucalyptus
> grove below the wet pasture,
> water's about hot,
> I sit in the open window
> & roll a smoke.

The same boy who wrote about 'Adlestrop' commented upon the relaxed stance of the poet here but also noted that there seemed to be an absence of anything but the personal diary-note: there was a lack of 'otherness' which informed the accumulation of detail in Thomas. The Wright poem provoked a more favourable response:

> Over my head, I see the bronze butterfly,
> Asleep on the black trunk,
> Blowing like a leaf in green shadow.
> Down the ravine behind the empty house,
> The cowbells follow one another
> Into the distances of the afternoon.
> To my right,
> In a field of sunlight between two pines,
> The droppings of last year's horses
> Blaze into golden stones.
> I lean back, as the evening darkens and comes on.
> A chicken-hawk floats over, looking for home.
> I have wasted my life.

Some of the group rather liked the juxtaposition of stillness and

movement, the poet's 'lying in a hammock' listening to the movement of 'cowbells' which provide a sense of 'distances'. However,
there was a growing feeling among the class that this was all rather
artificial. Why should the poet feel that he has wasted his life? I
suggested that they turn up Thomas's 'Digging':

Today I think
Only with scents,—scents dead leaves yield,
And bracken, and wild carrot's seed,
And the square mustard field;

Odours that rise
When the spade wounds the roots of tree,
Rose, currant, raspberry, or goutweed,
Rhubarb or celery;

The smoke's smell, too,
Flowing from where a bonfire burns
The dead, the waste, the dangerous,
And all to sweetness turns.

It is enough
To smell, to crumble the dark earth,
While the robin sings over again
Sad songs of Autumn mirth.

The comparison seemed just. Thomas's use of detail was more
complex and satisfying with that wry note of his which they were
learning to appreciate contained in the settled note of melancholy
and acceptance of the last line. Looking back again one of the
group pronounced the Americans as 'cold'.

It was with 'The Pond', or 'Bright Clouds' as it is sometimes
called, that the lessons shifted gear: we were looking at a poem
which was almost expressionist in form and redolent of the thought
process of a man waiting to go to war. We were suddenly made
aware that Thomas was a 'War Poet'. In 'The Pond' it was not
merely the 'Tall reeds/Like criss-cross bayonets' or the association
of may falling from the hawthorn with men dying in battle that
attracted attention; it was the power behind a word like 'frets' or
'drifts' which prompted us to look at other poetry of The First
World War. Most of the boys had come across some Owen and
Sassoon further down the school but what they didn't know was
Hardy's 'In Time of The Breaking of Nations' and we used the
quietness and almost self-conscious reflective voice ('a maid and
her wight') to refer back to Thomas's lines:

The light wind frets
And drifts the scum
Of may-blossom.

I also directed them to Alun Lewis who had been so influenced by
his reading of Thomas and noted for them the comments he made

in The Second World War about 'the rootless life of soldiers having
no enemy and always, somehow, under a shadow. . .' One boy
suggested that to be fair we should look at a Lewis poem rather
than just accept my brief quotation and so for the following lesson
I brought in 'To Edward Thomas'. We paused over the fourth
verse:

> Later, a whole day later, I remembered
> This war and yours and your weary
> Circle of failure and your striving
> To make articulate the groping voices
> Of snow and rain and dripping branches
> And love that ailing in itself cried out
> About the straggling eaves and ringed the candle
> With shadows slouching round your buried head;
> And in the lonely house there was no ease
> For you, or Helen, or those small perplexed
> Children of yours who only wished to please.

The 'striving/To make articulate' was noted as more personal and
direct than those cold details of Wright's or Snyder's. The picture
of Thomas the man seemed gently filled out by the reference to
Helen and the children and the mysterious quality shadowing his
verse was hinted at in such a way as to provoke the class to want
to find out more.

The next group of three poems which we looked at as specific
responses to the war were 'The Owl', 'Rain', and 'As the team's
head-brass'. This last we found occupied our attention more than
the others initially and proved to be a useful introduction to the
conversational style of writing adopted by Thomas in response to
Robert Frost's advice. Naturally enough the group wanted to know
more about the American, albeit with a slight feeling of distrust:
they were getting to feel a sense of loyalty towards Thomas! So we
spent a lesson looking at 'After Apple-Picking' and 'Mending Wall'
which served as a useful contrast enabling us to see how Thomas
used the conversational mode to convey not only the exactness of
a dramatic moment but also the quiet, reflective effect of the war
upon people at home. Doubtless on account of their early reading
of Owen and Sassoon they wanted Thomas to be indignantly
symbolic and so pressed for a limited reading of the last lines of
'As the team's head-brass':

> The horses started and for the last time
> I watched the clods crumble and topple over
> After the ploughshare and the stumbling team.

They insisted upon the image of men falling in the battle-field in
relation to 'last time', 'topple over' and 'stumbling'. So, in order
to wean them onto a wider perspective I brought into the next

lesson Hardy's 'During Wind and Rain' and it didn't take them long to register the positive irony behind the word 'ploughs' in the last line:

Down their carved names the raindrop ploughs.

Going back to the Thomas they were then less insistent upon a simple analogy between the actions of a ploughshare and the trenches of Flanders. We agreed that certainly there was a sense of disrupted cycles: the elm has 'fallen', the ploughman's mate is dead, the halting rhythm is disruptive and the plough itself is sufficiently martial with 'flashed', 'scraping', 'screwed' and 'treading me down'. However, the lovers constitute another reality as does the action of ploughing and both contain positive implications for the future.

About a month had now gone by and we were getting a fairly definite picture of Thomas's preoccupations and styles but there was obviously still much to do. Over the following two weeks we continued with the conversational poems, notably 'Up in the Wind' and 'May 23' and saw how they differed from the personally urgent tone of 'To Helen'. We examined the restless preoccupation with death in 'Lights Out' and 'The Other'. In order to detect the poetic quality of Thomas's handling of thought and language I finally referred them to comparisons between his prose and the poetry. The following extract from *The Icknield Way* highlighted in an excellent manner Thomas's stylistic development when we compared it with 'Rain':

I lay awake listening to the rain, and at first it was as pleasant to my ear and my mind as it had long been desired; but before I fell asleep it had become a majestic and finally terrible thing, instead of a sweet sound and symbol. It was accusing and trying me and passing judgement. Long I lay still under the sentence, listening to the rain, and then at last listening to words which seemed to be spoken by a ghostly double beside me. He was muttering; the all-night rain puts out summer like a torch. In the heavy, black rain falling straight from invisible, dark sky to invisible, dark earth the heat of summer is annihilated, the splendour is dead, the summer is gone. The midnight rain buries it away where it has buried all sound but its own . . . Sleep as all things, past, present, and future, lie still and sleep, except the rain the heavy, black rain falling straight through the air that was once a sea of life. That was a dream only. The truth is that the rain falls for ever and I am melting into it. Black and monotonously sounding is the midnight and solitude of the rain. In a little while or in an age—for it is all one— I shall know the full truth of the words I used to love, I knew not why, in my days of nature, in the days before the rain: 'Blessed are the dead that the rain rains on.'

Similarly the diary-note of 'Old Man's Beard' which is quoted in William Cooke's *A Critical Biography*, made a fine contrast to the poem with which we had started some weeks back. I now found it appropriate to look at a poem which I had steered clear of until

Ian Brinton

now, 'Words'. I felt that the poem about language would now mean something after we had seen the various examples of the poet's language in action. Words

> Worn new
> Again and again:
> Young as our streams
> After rain:
> And as dear
> As the earth which you prove
> That we love.

The regenerative power of Edward Thomas's language shone in a way that I was less sanguine of six weeks previously.

Bibliography

The Collected Poems of Edward Thomas, edited by R. George Thomas, Oxford University Press, 1981.

F. R. Leavis, *New Bearings in English Poetry*, Chatto, 1932 (reprinted in Peregrine Books, 1963).

Helen Thomas, *As It Was* and *World Without End*, London, 1956 (reprinted by Faber, 1978).

John Moore, *The Life and Letters of Edward Thomas*, London, 1939 (reprinted by Alan Sutton, 1984).

William Cooke, *Edward Thomas, A Critical Biography*, Faber, 1970.

Eleanor Farjeon, *Edward Thomas: The Last Four Years*, London, 1958.

R. George Thomas, *Edward Thomas, A Portrait*, Oxford University Press, 1985.

Edward Thomas, *The Childhood of Edward Thomas*, Faber, 1938 (reprinted by Faber, 1983).

Gary Snyder, *The Back Country*, Fulcrum, 1967.

Contemporary American Poetry, edited by Donald Hall, Penguin, 1971.

Selected Poems of Alun Lewis, Unwin, 1981.

Edward Thomas, *The Icknield Way*, Constable, 1913 (re-issued by Wildwood House Ltd. 1980).

JOSEPH HELLER: THERE'S ONLY ONE CATCH . . .

GERALD GIBBS

. . . and that's *Catch-22*. The novel that delighted and infuriated me in the early sixties, which seemed so relevant to our situation and to the war in Vietnam, is now one of the examination texts. I wondered whether or not to choose it: it has been on my sixth-form reading list for twenty years; those who tackled it loved it or hated it, and most the latter were girls. My 'A' level groups are composed mainly of girls—would it be fair to impose my enthusiasm on them, willy-nilly? And would the novel that seemed so relevant then seem at all relevant to the children of the eighties? Before deciding I first of all reread the novel, for the fourth time, and the conviction grew again: here was a major work. It seemed much more compelling than *Gulliver's Travels*, to which it was compared in the reviews and which I was teaching to another group. I passed a copy to one of my best students, who had just finished her examinations, but she could not get into it: 'the cover's too dull, the text's too small, the reviews too ecstatic', she told me. Nor was I at all sure that I understood the novel well enough to make a convincing job of teaching it, but I took the decision to go ahead, and spent the first week of the summer holiday annotating the text. The deeper I probed, the more it all seemed to cohere: even the most bizarre questions, such as 'Why is Nately's whore's kid sister beating Orr over the head with her shoe?' had answers. Having worked through the novel, I looked for critical work. John Wain's pioneering essay was encouraging but not specific enough, and I consulted two student guides: the Brodie guide by Graham Handley offers little more than brief chapter summaries and definitions of such terms as Babe Ruth, which are in Webster's Dictionary, and the Coles notes, by Joseph Blakey, which gives helpful but not entirely accurate notes on the structure of the novel—what he refers to as the first section ends at chapter eighteen, not seventeen, and the time sequence is easier to sort out than he suggests.

Most helpful was Robert Protherough's essay 'The Sanity of Catch-22' which makes the point that the novel is 'only in a limited way concerned with the war in its dissection of a whole range of contemporary attitudes and its queries about human nature and purpose'. He challenges Wain's assertion that the novel is circular, but rightly claims that it is progressive, for at the climax we see that Yossarian, 'instead of living in a continual present . . . finally discerns a connection between past, present and future and takes decisive action'. The later novels of Joseph Heller are less complex in structure than his first, but reinforce the themes of *Catch-22*: *Something Happened* is the most distinguished of its successors, and gives us Bob Slocum, trapped in a nightmarish bureaucratic complex in the office where he works, unable to understand why his family life has soured; *God Knows* presents us with the dying King David trying to make sense of his life—why did Saul hate him? why is God silent on the death of his son—how far can we be our family's, or our fellow-airman's, keeper? The characters in *Catch-22* seek to make sense of the system, but in *God Knows* even God disclaims any responsibility to make sense of the world— 'Show me where it says I have to make sense . . . I'll give milk, I'll give honey. Not sense.' The idea that *Catch-22* is a novel only about war was reinforced by the film version made in 1970 by Mike Nichols, who made the death of Snowden all-important, whereas in the novel it is the climax of a long chain of smaller events that combine to make Yossarian jump. The careful build-up of frustrations which face Yossarian in the novel, frustrations endemic to the multi-national impersonal businesses which were fore-shadowed by the war effort and Milo Minderbinder's ubiquitous capitalist enterprises and which face Slocum in the later novel, are lost in the film.

When preparing to teach the novel the first problem to resolve was the time sequence, and here I adapted Blakey's scheme. If we take as our base lines the hospitalisations of Yossarian, then the present time of the novel is his second stay, after the Avignon mission, and the next eighteen chapters can be taken as Yossarian filtering out the important events of his past, ending with the impersonation of Guiseppe at the cadet training school. From chapter nineteen onwards we are mainly in the present time, except for key events such as the death of Snowden, in the past, and the escape of Orr, in the future, which are recurring motifs in the action. Blakey is concerned that he cannot fit Milo's career into his scheme: I would argue that Milo is the least realistic of the characters, opening simultaneous enterprises in Sicily, Malta and Baghdad. The major characters realise that they are trapped by the military and capitalist systems, and stand against them; as Yossarian puts it, 'Someone has to do something sometime'. Catch-22 itself, the law which ensures that no-one can beat the system, is eventually seen to be a 'con' perpetrated to keep the wheels in motion; Yossarian could have learned this at cadet school, when the doctor told him it was all illusion, but it only comes home to

him in the wrecked whorehouse in Rome: 'Catch-22 did not exist,
he was positive of that, but it made no difference.' It takes Yossarian the whole of the novel to realise the truth he saw in the
dying Snowden, that 'man is matter', and that he must make the
most of his brief existence in a world in which he can 'see people
cashing in on every decent impulse and human tragedy'. The novel
presents three possible responses to the situation: to opt out, as
the chaplain is tempted to do, until he realises that opting out
'merely required no character'; to opt in, and battle for promotion,
as most of the minor characters do; or to 'jump' out of the situation
altogether and try to make a fresh start, as Orr does, as Clevinger
may have done, and as Yossarian tries to do in the final paragraph
of the novel. The good characters share a certain lacklustre quality,
an inability to put their worthy impulses into action: Major Major
has a genuine concern for the enlisted men, but cannot act out that
concern because of his administrative incompetence; the chaplain,
agonising over his ability to accept his Fundamentalist beliefs, is
eventually compelled by his conscience to take a stand beside
Yossarian; other, weaker characters restrict their support to just
approaching him under cover of darkness to express their admir-
ation of him. Heller shows clearly that in multi-layered systems
it is the 'minor' persons who wield most real power: ex-PFC
Wintergreen takes it upon himself to decide which orders are
published, according to the prose style of the Generals; Sergeant
Towser makes the decisions for Major Major, and Corporal Whit-
comb acts on behalf of the chaplain, though he goes too far in
his condolence letter in its 'delete where appropriate' format.
Yossarian tries to change the system from within, but fails; Orr,
as the name suggests, embodies an alternative philosophy of 'taking
off' and rowing to what he hopes will be freedom in Sweden. That
freedom may be no more than the freedom from war, but both he
and Yossarian know that the system they leave behind is too
corrupt to be changed.

   Having sorted out my own responses to the book, I then taught
it to a very lively class which did not take my opinions over without
testing them severely first. I gave them the novel to read over the
summer, and asked them to write a plot summary in chronological
sequence. They all struggled to do this, some of them going straight
to Brodies or Coles notes and reproducing the contradictions there.
These notes can be helpful in summarising a long and complex
novel, particularly for revision purposes, but I never recommend
them directly to pupils—they find them easily enough! The first
problem tackled in class, in groups, was to work out what actually
happens, and when, in the novel; we did this by plunging into
the middle of it, to Chapter twenty-one, 'General Dreedle', and

expanding Colonel Cathcart's list of 'black eyes and feathers in my cap'; from this central point we could move forwards and backwards in the novel. Then I asked what the novel was about—did it have a universal significance? And here I directed pupils to *Something Happened*, and I read them the first ten pages. We concluded that the novel is about people caught up in a system from which there is no escape—even Orr's escape they felt was illusory—unless one opts for the nightmare breakdown world of the eternal present that Yossarian inhabits in the first half of the novel. We imagined how other characters might view Yossarian, wrote a letter to Pianosa from Orr in Sweden, and wrote character studies in pairs. One very useful exercise was to see which chapters of the book could be edited out without loss: this led us to see the novel as a seamless garment, and sharpened our sense of how good a writer Heller is. After ten weeks on the novel, we watched the film, and the general opinion was that the film was much better than I had led them to expect. The essays they wrote indicate their responses. Catherine took a long time to come to terms with the seriousness of Heller's intentions:

> Though he does not say so outright, Heller's constant implications that the novel is derived from the truth are most obvious (one would say about as obvious as a bull in a china shop) and do perhaps go a little way to compensate for the fact that little or no enjoyment may be gained from the novel.

Sarah had just completed a holiday project on responses to war in diaries, poems and autobiographies, and was quick to place Heller in a tradition:

> *Catch-22* is written by a man possessing primary evidence, but writing the book some time after the event. Are his emotions, therefore, 'hot' and realistic? Can the reader look at the book as a reflection of the emotion and general feeling of the time? One thing is quite clear, that Heller's use of satire is strongly felt; the feeling of resentment and hostility will burn inside him for evermore.

Richard, to go on to study law, was adept at taking my miserable essay titles to the cleaner's—usually I invented a quotation and invited discussion of it, as in ' "One of the main targets of Heller's satire is the incompetence of the officers." Discuss.'

> The title is quite misleading. The target of Heller's satire is not so much individual incompetence as the system it reflects. The officers are instruments of the satire, not targets; it is they who illuminate the ridiculous nature of that which surrounds the airbase, and that which infuriates the author to write. There are many examples of the author using individuals to point fun and to make particular targets look ridiculous. The three main targets of the satire are: the medical profession, the 'war machine' itself, and the bureaucracy.

One aspect on which we all eventually agreed was that it was well-written—outstandingly so in the terrifyingly real action sequences with the bombardier in his 'goldfish bowl' above the flak. Sarah again:

> There is a feeling of panic in the writing about the raid on Avignon—virtually a
> whole paragraph without punctuation, words underlined by alliteration and
> onomatopoeia—and the reader is left gasping for breath.

Discussion of the bureaucratic nature of school life proved fruitful, especially when we realised that school discipline is a Catch-22 situation, a set of rules that cannot realistically be applied; and we all could name sixth-formers who had been 'disappeared'! As Michelle pointed out, it is easy to succumb to the system, and it can give a feeling of belonging that can console the weakest link— 'Even ex-PFC Wintergreen,' she wrote, 'of lowest rank, when asked what would happen if an order was disobeyed, said, "*We* would shoot you." '

The ending of the novel provoked the most argument. What should Yossarian have done? Should he have allowed himself to be disappeared back to the States, and then bucked the system from his position of superiority? Matthew passionately argued that the 'jump' to freedom was no real way out at all, that Yossarian would have found Sweden even more oppressive than America. Others in the group agreed with Colonel Korn that Yossarian would accept the rewards he was offered when he returned home: 'You'll enjoy a rich, rewarding, luxurious, privileged existence. You'd have to be a fool to throw it all away just for a moral principle, and you're not a fool', as Korn reminds him. By the end of the novel we also agreed that the comic names of the characters had been off-putting: they are much more 'real' than the first impressions had suggested. Teaching *Catch-22* proved an enjoyable and stimulating experience: we had been on a journey of discovery together. Revision work on the novel, immediately prior to the examination, was, as is often the case, much less enjoyable. In two weeks of revision we concentrated on the major characters of the novel—Yossarian, Major Major and Milo—and on the structure, and our efforts were rewarded by the Board giving the candidates a choice between two very straightforward questions: 'What positive values, if any, does Heller present through the character of Yossarian in *Catch-22*? Illustrate in detail from the novel', and 'What do you consider the advantages and disadvantages of the structure of *Catch-22*?'

Pleased with my success in teaching the novel for the first time, I decided to teach it again with the following year's lower sixth, and with much more confidence than I had felt earlier. I was surprised to find that the enthusiasm of the first group was not shared by the second: the chemistry of the group did not seem to take to Heller's sense of humour, and for a long time the pupils

failed to see the novel as a comic one. Perhaps we missed the
quirky sense of humour that was manifested by half a dozen of the
first group, many of whom had progressed to other of Heller's
novels and to Kurt Vonnegut's *Slaughterhouse 5*; or did the fault
lie more with me? The sense of discovery had gone, the questions
that had so industriously been tackled by the first group had
now been answered, and their long-running query, about Nately's
whore's kid sister, did not generate the same competitive spirit in
the finding of the answer. I tackled the novel in the same way as
before, but revision work proved more difficult; having spotted
two questions the first time round I found it difficult to imagine
what the examiners could ask in the next questions. Our revision
this time concentrated on an analysis of the major scenes in the
novel (each of us choosing a comic scene and a tragic scene to
present to the rest of the group) and we each chose a minor
character—Orr, Dunbar, Nately's whore, Snowden, for example—
and explained why the character played an important role in the
plot, and tried to analyse motives. The examination questions
proved much more difficult: '*Catch-22* is more than an anti-war
novel' seemed straightforward, but only the better candidates
grasped that Heller's analysis of the society on Pianosa could be
applied to western society in general, and only those who had read
and understood *Something Happened* could answer this with any
confidence; the second question consisted of four fairly lengthy
quotations from the novel, all of them dealing with the death of
Snowden, the recurring nightmare which is the final cause of
Yossarian's breakdown, with this question: 'Use the following four
passages to comment on the impact, style and narrative methods
of Heller's *Catch-22*. (The chapters are identified by numbers and
characters' names, as in the text. You may also refer to other
passages of your own choice if you wish).' There are various
problems raised by questions such as this: the time taken to read
the passages discourages some of the slower readers, and I suspect
that most of my candidates who tackled this question wrote about
the character and death of Snowden, because this is how we had
tackled Snowden in our revision, rather than about the style and
narrative methods that were asked for by the question. Although
we had looked hard at style and narrative method, only the more
capable pupils found these easy to write about.

Students from the two groups who have come back to school to
tell me of their progress have often talked of their reading: many
of the first group have read other books by Joseph Heller—
Matthew had read all of them, and persuaded relatives to buy him
copies of Heller's books as Christmas and birthday presents—and
followed his writing career with great interest; only one of the

second group read anything else by Heller. The contrast between the ways in which the two groups responded to the same text made me reflect upon my own part in the process: while I was researching *Catch-22* and exploring the novel to find answers to the many questions raised by the first group my own interest and enthusiasm was infectious; the second group's lack of a matching enthusiasm may have been, in part, due to my own sense that the novel was a closed book. It is interesting to note, finally, that the examination results of the two groups were not significantly different: *Catch-22* was only one text out of seven, but the results suggest that enthusiasm is not an ingredient which is well rewarded at Advanced Level.

References

John Wain's essay is to be found in *The Critical Quarterly*, Volume 5, (ii) (Manchester University Press).
Robert Protherough's essay is in *The Human World*, number 3. (Brynmill Press).
An interesting and different view of teaching *Catch-22* can be found in the essay by Judith Atkinson in *Teaching Literature for Examinations*, edited by Robert Protherough (Open University Press).

PHILIP LARKIN: THE WHITSUN WEDDINGS, *Or* THE SYLLABUS WITH A HOLE IN IT

Bryan Robson

What *is* poetry? We can see what it *was*—but what is it now? Still 'a criticism of life'? 'Memorable speech'? Or words and thoughts that '. . . wear down to their simplest sense,/Yet remain'? Whatever it is poetry, according to Philip Larkin, 'chose' him—he'd have preferred to go on writing novels, but couldn't get interested enough in other people: poetry is more about 'yourself'.

Jill, Larkin's first novel, concerns John Kemp, a lonely scholarship boy from the north, at Oxford during the second world war. Driven into isolation by the coarse sophistication of the public-schoolboys who surround him, Kemp withdraws to fantasy, inventing a sister, Jill, for whom he imagines a detailed existence at a smart boarding-school. After losing himself in novelistic writing about 'Jill', Kemp is astonished at coming across the girl he has imagined, in a bookshop. She turns out to be the sixteen-year-old cousin of his room-mate's girl-friend. Kemp becomes obsessed by the real Jill.

Later in the book Kemp is returning by train to Oxford after a panic visit to his home, following reports of devastating air-raids. He has found his home intact but deserted, his parents safe; nevertheless the havoc wrought by the bombing has impressed him deeply.

> He was tired, and what he had seen had made him feel as negligible as a fly crawling over a heap of stones: it made life seem like an unsuccessful attempt to light a candle in the wind . . . .
> The galloping wheels insinuated their unrest into his dreams, he saw once again the scarecrow buildings, the streets half heaved-up by detonations . . . It no longer seemed meaningless: struggling awake again . . . he thought it . . . symbolic, a kind of annulling of his childhood. The thought excited him. It was as if he had been told: all the past is cancelled: all the suffering connected with that town, all your childhood, is wiped out. Now there is a fresh start for you: you are no longer governed by what has gone before.
> The train ran on, through fields lying under the frost and darkness.
> And then again, it was like being told: see how little anything matters. All that anyone has is the life that keeps him going, and see how easily that can be patted out. See how appallingly little life is.
> He yawned and grinned, clasping his hands between his knees.[1]

That episode makes an apt curtain-raiser to the class's reading of 'Dockery and Son': its connection with the train journey setting of the two most substantial poems in *The Whitsun Weddings* can hardly be coincidental. Of course, the illusory quality of Kemp's sense of liberation, its denial by the story's remaining events, might be guessed by anyone familiar with the poetry. Mr Bleaney's successor (Kemp hurrying on down?) *grinned and shivered*, telling himself that this 'hired box' was 'home'.[2] Poems don't make people actually jump out of windows, but Larkin's words (often insinuating and reasonable as the language of Swift's *Modest Proposal*) can stun young readers into depression. 'Slow dying'. 'The solving emptiness' . . . 'First boredom, then fear'. 'It seems that what Larkin should be saying (one of the first-years complained) is, "My life was first boredom, now it's fear"'. He doesn't need to generalise and inflict his views on our lives.'

So—should we be teaching *The Whitsun Weddings*?

Not everyone would see that as an intelligible question. Wasn't Larkin Betjeman-approved? 'Simply the best poet writing in English'?[3] At the same time, 'What *can* be said for Larkin?' Brian Lee wanted to know three years after his 'Haltwhistle Quarterly' assault on Larkin's standing as 'our best man': 'something perhaps, but to calculate the quantity would be a nice task.'[4]

> This is the first thing
> I have understood:
> Time is the echo of an axe
> Within a wood.

('XXVI', The North Ship,)[5]

Larkin's sense that life is negated by its final extinction 'to some/ Means nothing;/others it leaves/Nothing to be said.' But you can't read Larkin and *not* hear that 'echo'. 'If you assume you're going to live to be seventy, seven decades, and think of each decade as a day of the week . . . Rather a shock, isn't it?'[6] And in the interim (as "Ignorance" would have us believe)'[7] . . . to know nothing, never to be sure/Of what is true or right or real . . .?' Well, someone, surely, was right to have a go at that and other defeatisms in this widely-known poetry? 'I really want to hit them (Larkin told the "Observer" Review), 'I want readers to feel yes, I've never thought of it that way, but that's how it is.'

Larkin can't have exulted in becoming a syllabus poet ('I should hate anyone to read my work because he's been told to and told what to think about it'), but a number of jumped at the chance of spending time on *The Whitsun Weddings* with a class. What fun we had, surprising in ourselves a hunger to be more undeceived: about how 'unearthly love is,/Or women are' ('The Large Cool Store'), about how love can't 'solve or satisfy' ('Love Songs in

Age'), how marriage is a joyous shot that goes wide ('Home is so Sad') and about assumptions that harden into 'all we've got and how we got it' ('Dockery and Son').

Before the end of our course I knew that something sufficiently Larkinlike squatted in me too, soiling a good portion of the week with its sad, clever irony and vengeful jokes. Instead of taking the brute's spiritual arm I tried driving it off with parody, encouraging my class to do the same, until Brian Lee (in the article I've referred to) convinced me that 'if you like Larkin a lot it is a bad sign for you': 'Self-pity, Society, Sentimentality, Satire . . . *how do we get out of it?*' Not by addicting ourselves to the shrugs, defensive ironies, evasions, wry puzzlement, moping and so on in Larkin— Lee *places* these as *sentimentality*—'the literary word for moaning'—and worse:

> What do we write poems *for*, but for life; what do we read poems for, but for life? And here is our best man from whom you come away feeling, on the whole, a bit more like death: who keeps on saying that there's nothing to be said.[9]

We went back over some poems (it was like substituting negative for print). How knowingly, through Larkin's railway-carriage window, we'd spotted the 'cut-price crowd' ('Here') and patronised the wedding parties on midlands platforms ('The Whitsun Weddings'). And why should I have expected my pupils, their 'apple' of life mostly unbitten in the palm ('As Bad as a Mile'), to see as grown-up and sophisticated that travestying of 'truth' as a 'trite, untransferable truss-advertisement' ('Send No Money')? How truthful had *I* been when I disagreed yes-no-ishly with Larkin's assumption that 'adding' (wife, children) 'meant dilution'?—did I see myself as ending up with 'what something hidden' from me chose ('Dockery and Son')?

And if we'd enjoyed all those jokes that much—too late to wish we hadn't: 'Well, useful to get that learnt' ('Wild Oats') . . . 'Granny Graveclothes' Tea' ('Essential Beauty') . . . 'Cemetery Road' ('Toads Revisited') . . . '*first boredom, then fear . . .*' Outrageously funny—or plain outrageous? I looked up for them what Auden makes Prospero say, in *The Sea and the Mirror*: 'Can I learn to suffer/Without saying something ironic or funny/About suffering?'[10] And I wish I could have tacked on Larkin's anecdote (interview, 'Paris Review' 1980) of his meeting Auden, once. 'I remember he said, Do you like living in Hull? and I said, I don't suppose I'm any unhappier there than I should have been anywhere else. To which he replied, Naughty, naughty. I thought that was very funny.' (Ah, yes. And perhaps Auden meant it).

So (with Larkin's recent death to alter the perspective again) it happens that I have returned to *The Whitsun Weddings*, wondering, as before, if it would have made me, at seventeen, think to any purpose—or at all—about girls and women, or what to aim at: about what Johnson's Rasselas eagerly calls the *choice of life*[11]— that illusive option on which *The Whitsun Weddings* harps in such doleful, minor keys. Will these boys emerge to share Larkin's advocated rejection of self-surrender, of marriage (e.g. in 'Self's the Man')? *Our flesh surrounds us with its own decisions* ('Ignorance'). Poetry, Auden said, can make nothing happen and nothing (Larkin adds) 'like something, happens anywhere'.[12]

At sixteen-plus most in the class know a Larkin poem or two— 'At Grass', 'Myxomatosis', 'Wires' (All in *The Less Deceived* 1952) and 'MCMXIV' *(Whitsun Weddings)* are likeliest: Before widening 'Titch Thomas'''s circle of friends ('Sunny Prestatyn') I introduce the uncollected poetry/language manifesto, 'Modesties' which appeared in 'Encounter', March 1964:

> Words as plain as hen-birds' wings
> Do not lie,
> Do not over-broider things,
> Are too shy.

> Thoughts that shuffle round like pence
> From reign to reign
> Wear down to their simplest sense,
> Yet remain . . .

Pupils are prone to neglect the rhetorically seductive effects of Larkin's language which often nerve their response (considering 'Days' a boy wrote . . . 'The very sound of the word 'days' repeated in the poem is monotonous but not soothing'). The artful lyricism of his rhythms ranges from the old-overcoat warmth of blank verse ('Canal and colleges and clouds subside') to Audenesque octosyllabics ('Such faithfulness in effigy/Was just a detail friends would see') and shifts to the clipped and abrasive 'Come to *Sunny Prestatyn*' and 'Evil was just my lark . . . Get stewed./Books are a load of crap'—lines which are disingenuous rather than 'plain' and where the writ of 'modesty' doesn't quite run.

A few questions surface here. He that beguiles you in a plain accent is a plain knave, so—where's the sense of 'Do not lie'? and what sort of words 'over-broider' things (a recherché word itself)? Why should we trust thoughts that are worn and commonplace, like old pennies? What about that use of analogy as argument? and 'where', as another poem will ask, 'do these innate assumptions come from'?[13]

We look at 'Here'. Why not start with the title poem? someone asks. I suggest: Because it's in the middle of the book. It occurs to met that *The Whitsun Weddings* cannot be read like a novel: with its score of 'visions and revisions' it is plotted, all right—but not in the sense that *Jill* is. Then nor is it a random collection, an anthology. It is, however one judges it, a book, a coherent sequence of imaginings. But—to suggest this to the class is close to telling them what to think. It may do better, at least, retrospectively. 'Here' is always full of interest: a 'swerving' travelogue of Humberside and beyond, to the poet's destination 'on the edge of things'.

> And out beyond its mortgaged half-built edges
> Fast-shadowed wheat-fields, running high as hedges,
> Isolate villages, where removed lives
>
> Loneliness clarifies. Here silence stands
> Like heat.

We talk about views from the train. Some boys assume Larkin was in a car or on a coach: 'halts' is unfamiliar, 'stealing flat-faced trolleys' unguessable (some can connect the phrase only with the supermarket). We consider 'raw estates' (urban sprawl?), 'pastorals of ships up streets' and get on to . . . 'Loneliness clarifies . . . unfenced existence:/Facing the sun, untalkative, out of reach.'

Ideas start to flow from this, the language making it pretty clear where the poet's sympathies lie, in the lingering rhythmic pull towards 'remote lives' as (somehow) benign and real. A mulling pause. 'He's a bit anti-social then', a boy decides. Well, one way of looking at it. .

'Absences' (from *The Less Deceived*) and Hardy's 'Wessex Heights' offer comparison with 'Here' and reading them at this point can make an essay-skirmish into 'Here' a less cramped sort of exercise. There are, naturally, other poems among the thirty-one in *The Whitsun Weddings* which stake out the ground rules of Larkin's poetic land—although in a sense they all do this and their feeling is cumulative, rather like (to borrow an idea Larkin noted with enjoyment, in his TV 'Monitor' appearance in 1964, about the Humber estuary) the gradual piling of cloud on cloud, catching a sunset.

That, on second thoughts, is too decorative—too over-broidered: one shouldn't waste sentiment. Perhaps the cumulativeness is more analogous to the 'coastal shelf' of misery which ('This Be the Verse', in *High Windows*) Larkin informs us man hands on to man (and woman too, one supposes).[14]

In an interview Larkin said he believed most people walk around with a sense of failure and unhappiness, but the poetry of *The Whitsun Weddings*, for all its efforts at tenderness (as in 'Love Songs in Age', 'Broadcast', 'An Arundel Tomb') creates its own log-jam of sadness and defeat. The continual attempts to set us against the illusions which Larkin sees as propping people's lives

up (see 'Mr. Bleaney', 'The Large Cool Store', 'Essential Beauty')
may win their debating-points amid wry laughter, but they keep
coming unstuck with anyone who gets real, even if intermittent,
pleasure out of being. But there I go again, almost forgetting that
I'd never allow myself (as a 'spectacled school-teaching sod')[15] to
prejudice a fair deal for Larkin by telling my class what to think.
Where do we go from 'Here'? Not far. To the next page in fact,
to survey the grim bedsitter Mr. Bleaney has vacated, in some car-
manufacturing *locale*. None of the class, despite days and months
of watching television, has much idea of how a 'Brum' or Coventry
landlady might sound. So I enjoy voicing her in tones that contrast
with the detached, drily-mutinous Larkin-voice in the poem.

Mr. Bleaney's room has the defeating drabness, carried over
from the 'austerity' 1940s into the 1950s, which is captured in films
like 'Waterloo Road' and 'London Belongs to Me'; in Kingsley
Amis's *Lucky Jim* and the early part of David Lodge's *Out of the
Shelter*. It's on the underside of that shilling-in-the-meter, string-
bag, illusion-stripped world of Barbara Pym's novels—of which
Larkin was a committed champion—in which emotion was
guarded, you had only what you could pay for and where few could
afford much (no 'cut-price crowd').

In fact, though, this has little enough to do with the 'dread/That
how we live measures our own nature' and head-downwards though
most in my class are in modern, not contemporary, reality, it is
unnecessary to explain why Larkin, Wain, Amis and others began
writing as they did.[16]

More interesting are Larkin's own statements—creative, critical
and autobiographical. Enough in the second and third categories
is accessible in *Required Writing*, a compendium published by
Faber, 1984. If one must narrow the choice for hard-pressed
candidates, Larkin's Introductions to the Faber reprints of *Jill* and
The North Ship (his earliest poetry) should be included at all cost.

Before tackling at length 'The Whitsun Weddings' and 'Dockery
and Son', I pair off some shorter poems and call for one detailed
written comparison: 'Broadcast' and 'Wild Oats' (baffled romanti-
cism); 'Days' and 'Ambulances'; 'Sunny Prestatyn' and 'Essential
Beauty' (a raspberry for the Ad-man). 'Toads Revisited' means
visiting 'Toads' (to be found in Larkin's second collection, *The
Less Deceived*, 1952). Most students will be quick to spot how the
wishful bravado of the earlier poem has been replaced with an
image of work-dodging as something not witty, but 'stupid or
weak'. There's a reflection of the techniques (para-rhyme) and
structure of 'Toads' but the earlier, differentiated, 'toads' have
now merged. It is the job itself which props Larkin up, for the
apparently meaningless short walk down 'Cemetery Road'.

I have to admit to having found this very funny ten years ago: now I seem to hear another voice croaking, Naughty, naughty. My class's reactions vary—they are growing up in a society which pays large numbers of people (university graduates among them) to be unemployed. But the assumption that life is about jobs (rooted in middle- as well as in working-class tradition) hasn't really changed.

'He appears to be reconciling [the fact] that his job is the best life can offer him. He condemns firstly those with no jobs and as Larkin sees it, no real lives at all.'
(First year sixth boy on 'Toads Revisited')

In fact, *The Whitsun Weddings* offers similar-tasting medicine to that of *The Less Deceived* for what is seen as an incurable condition. Why can't people get it 'permanent and blank and true'? the poems seem to ask: our notions about most things are—lies, a screening of our graves with custard—and love? well, either another illusion or else something almost unreachably privileged. Yes, Larkin is prepared to admit that our 'almost-instinct' may be 'almost-true'—

What will survive of *us* is love—

('An Arundel Tomb')

but won't imagine that the experience of being loved is not uncommon or unreal: because life is ignorance and illusion and (finally) defeat for him, the energy of all the newly-weds on the train at Whitsun is 'like an arrow-shower . . . somewhere becoming rain'. 'Marriage, he claims, is another step along Cemetery Road, a "happy funeral" ' (another first year boy). I'm glad to share Larkin's vision where I can—his nostalgia for 'Domesday' England and detestation of the ad-mass mess-up which is replacing it.[17] Against that I have to set this cosy, wrap-around acceptance of life as unhappiness and defeat—a view which, as the pupil just quoted moved on to say, 'indicates that Larkin appears to find no answer as to what life should be for, or that it needs any fun or enjoyment'.

And some of that analogy-argument too—that 'shied apple-core' for instance ('As Bad as a Mile'): what *qualitative* connection is there between that and, say, the failure in Arnold's miscalculation ('Self's the Man') about wanting to stop a woman from getting away; or in the sadness of 'home' ('Home is so Sad'), once children, after pushing their mothers 'to the side of their own lives' (according to 'Afternoons'), have deserted it? *There isn't any*, isn't meant to be: the apple-core is a reductive symbol, calculatedly trivialising and offensive.

No, unanswerable though poetry is, give me (in this mood) Kipling, whose thoughts on squaring up to failure shuffled round like pence through four reigns at least. Give me Dr Johnson, whose grasp of the real-vs-illusion and horror of extinction were palpable, but who loved 'to see a knot of little misses' and felt the death of the Thrales' son as one of the worst of personal tragedies. Johnson's 'marriage had many pains, but celibacy no pleasures' reads almost as a footnote to *The Whitsun Weddings* (but for its frank humour and certainty). Look up Johnson on that four-letter word 'Life', in the index volume of the great Oxford edition of Boswell's *Life of Johnson*:

> few have any choice of . . ./just choice impossible . . . composed of small incidents . . ./more to be endured that enjoyed . . ./'balance of misery' . . . 'nauseous draught' . . ./none would live it again . . . Etc.

Isn't that close enough to Larkin's 'Beneath it all desire of oblivion runs' ('Wants') to put it in perspective? Awareness of 'the solving emptiness/That lies just under all we do' is as real in *Rasselas* as it is in 'Ambulances', but Larkin won't keep it in hand, he'd rather it became the whole truth. 'Slow dying'. The axe in the wood. As another pupil sums it up:

> The emptiness of . . . existence is described throughout the collection and more particularly in 'Days' . . . ('They are to be happy in') he tells us that he has failed to fulfil this expectation of life.'

I began by tracing such attitudes and perceptions back to the almost undergraduate Larkin of his novels:

> But did she (Katherine in *A Girl in Winter*) really care what she did? . . . whatever it was she would do it unwillingly, obstinately, as if she were working in a field; what she did would be emptied away like a painfully-filled basket, and her time would be spilled away with it . . . and it did not matter if she accepted it or not. It accepted her.[18]

They were unrepented in 'The Life with a Hole in It'—

> Life is an immobile, locked
> Three-handed struggle between
> Your wants, the world's for you and, (worse)
> The unbeatable slow machine
> That brings you what you'll get . . .
> (*Poetry Supplement*, 1974, compiled by Larkin)

Relieved occasionally by half-tones, reasons to be cheerless pervade *The Whitsun Weddings.*—Where's the catch? my class wants to know, sceptical of what looks to be a gleam of optimism in 'First Sight': well, we aren't lambs, are we? (a realist reminds us)—remember the butcher. In 'For Sidney Bechet' (jazz mystique) it's the blue-notes which fall as a great yes like love.[19]

So should we be teaching *The Whitsun Weddings*? The question is hardly one that can be put to the class—the only people who can answer it for me. Each will have to talk about one or two poems, seminar-style, of his own choosing. Their 'required writing' will have entailed some thinking about the Larkin *catharsis*—the balance, let's say, of pity and terror: between our need to fend off the insidious, comprehensive unpicking of 'our' life, with all its 'imprecisions', and the out-reach of our imaginative sympathy to the poet's sadness, nostalgia, uncertainty and dread—or, if you prefer, the *drama* of those feelings displayed in the poems.

The nostalgia, perhaps, is what our pupils' finest response will identify and learn from: the strident bluster of 'Self's the Man' will show up as defensive and self-justifying, while the poignant story sketched in 'Wild Oats' (we aren't fooled by the self-ironic humour) has a sad truthfulness about it. The wistful, serious tone of 'An Arundel Tomb' brings the sequence to an almost yearning close.

There may even be a special value in 'teaching' a poet who inspires such mixed feelings: ambivalence is not inconsistency and can be communicated honestly as a part of reading. I'd be the first to admit that my own very different sorts of feeling about Larkin's poetry and its *tendency*, its meaning for us, are rather like his 'toads': it is hard to lose either when you have both.

References

1. Philip Larkin, *Jill* (1946). Faber 1975 edition, p. 219.
2. *The Whitsun Weddings* (in these notes subsequently TWW), p. 10. All references are to the Faber p/b edition of 1975.
3. Clive James (or someone very like him), 'Encounter', 1979.
4. Brian Lee, 'Larkin and Montale, Self-pity, Society, Sentimentality, Satire, or: how do we get out of it?' in 'The Haltwhistle Quarterly' No. 4 Spring 1976. Lack of space prevents me from doing justice to the astringent argument and style of Mr. Lee's revaluation. 'What can be said . . .?' etc. came up in an exchange of correspondence in 1979.
5. Philip Larkin, *The North Ship* (1946). Reprinted by Faber, 1974.
6. At the time of this interview, with Miriam Gross, in 1979, Larkin said he was now on 'Friday afternoon'.
7. TWW, p. 39.
8. All in TWW.
9. 'Haltwhistle Quarterly' No. 4, p. 9.
10. W. H. Auden, *For the Time Being*, Faber 1945, p. 15.
11. Samuel Johnson, *The History of Rasselas, Prince of Abyssinia*, Penguin edition.
12. See 'I Remember, I Remember . . .' *(The Less Deceived)*.
13. 'Dockery and Son', TWW, p. 38.
14. See 'This be the Verse'—one of the poems which ruled Larkin out as Poet Laureate-elect.
15. See 'The Life with a Hole in It', *Poetry Supplement*, compiled by Larkin for the Poetry Society, 1974.
16. See Blake Morrison, *The Movement*, O.U.P., 1980.
17. See especially 'Going, going . . .' in *High Windows*, 1974.
18. Philip Larkin, *A Girl in Winter* (1947), Faber edition, 1957, p. 216.
19. The rhetoric is hard to resist: jazz makes all come clear. The 'snivel on the violins' and 'cascades of monumental slithering' which sustain the girl at the concert (see 'Broadcast') are a more deluding experience, one can't help supposing.

ALICE WALKER: *THE COLOR PURPLE*

MICHAEL WILLIAMS

Alice Walker's *The Color Purple* was published in the United States in 1982, and in Britain in 1983.[1] The novel has achieved a significant popular success, which has been further promoted by Steven Spielberg's cinematic adaptation.[2] In the United States, *The National Leader* (7/10/82) described its author as 'a Resounding Voice for Black Women'; *The New York Times Magazine* (8/1/84) credited Alice Walker as 'Telling the Black Woman's Story'; and she herself has been honoured in the States with a Radcliffe Institute *Fellow*ship(!), a Guggenheim *Fellow*ship, and a Creative Writing Award from the National Endowment for the Arts. In England, the novel has appeared on an 'A' Level Syllabus in double-quick time. In *The Use of English* (Autumn 1987: p. 69), Gillian Spraggs posed the question with reference to 'A' Level syllabi: 'When will we see Alice Walker alongside Scott Fitzgerald?' Time has overtaken her question because *The Color Purple* has appeared on the AEB 'A' Language and Literature Syllabus for examination in Summer 1989.

The novel is in epistolary form—a fact which evokes the rôle played by female writers in the early development of the English Novel. The main character, Celie, writes to God, who never replies, about her experiences of incestuous child rape by her supposed father, and the supposed disposal (one killed, and one sold) of her two children/brother and sister; her voluntary self-sacrifice to save her younger sister, Nettie, not only from their 'father', who has lost interest in Celie and is pestering the younger child, but also from a neighbour, Mr. ———, (later known as Albert), who wants to marry Nettie, but accepts Celie instead; her sister's running away; her husband's assertion of his 'right' to beat her; her growing involvement with her husband's mistress, Shug Avery, a singer in the tradition of Bessie Smith; her observation of the relationship between her step-son, Harpo, and his wife, Sofia, and Sofia's atrocious treatment by the local white authorities; her shocking discovery that over a period of many years her husband has been hiding letters from her sister, Nettie, which she reads . . . to discover that her 'father' was in fact her step-father, and that her children are not dead or sold, but alive and well and living with a missionary family and her sister in Africa. Eventually the letters record a reconstruction of Celie's family life, but in the novel's final settlement of Celie's relationships, there is a clear demotion of monogamy, the nuclear family, and heterosexuality.

Clearly, the novel's impact depends largely on Alice Walker's success in creating the effect of an authentic black folk speech written down. This is a feature which even critics who have expressed the severest reservations about the novel have recognised and praised:

> Celie's voice in the novel is powerful, engaging, subtly humorous, and incisively analytic at the basic level of human interactions. The voice is perfectly suited to the character, and Walker has breathed into it a vitality that frequently over-shadows the problematic areas of concern in the novel.[3]

In September, 1987, I followed my usual practice with an incoming 'A' Level group, and issued the nine students (eight girls, one boy) with copies of most of the set books prescribed for AEB Language and Literature. I invited them to start reading with a view to negotiating a selection of the texts for study. *The Color Purple* appeared on Paper 2, and was an instant 'hit'. Within several weeks, there was no doubt that it would appear in the final selection of texts for examination in Summer 1989.

I had originally planned to base the study of the novel on a written agenda, outlining areas of inquiry, and suggesting questions and activities relating to them.

The following areas were what I originally proposed: the novel's 'canonization' by the media; its possible reinforcement of racialist stereotypes; Alice Walker's treatment of men; Celie's 'voice'; possible tensions between the imagined experience and the chosen discursive mode; elements of Fairy Tale and questions of Fantasy; the relevance of the African sections; Lesbianism; Celie's growth and development; the genesis of *Color Purple* as described by Alice Walker. I arranged the areas for study in what I hoped would be a logical progression which would support not only the students but also myself in what was, at that point, fairly unknown teaching territory. I wanted to start by examining how Alice Walker had come to displace and succeed other black writers, notably James Baldwin and Toni Morrison, in critical esteem. I saw that as leading into questions of racism in the critical acclaim, whereby the white-dominated media might perhaps have selected for esteem a text which could be read as a reinforcement of racialist stereotypes. That would then lead to a consideration of whether the men in the novel were not uncomfortably close to the sexually dangerous animals caricatured, say, by the Ku Klux Klan. That could then lead to an examination of Alice Walker's creation of Celie's voice, and the extent to which we are engaging in a highly individual history and not a generalisation about black life. Looking at the question of 'voice' might then raise the question of the credibility of an initially illiterate girl *writing* to God. Looking at elements of Fairy Tale and Fantasy could be a useful way of reflecting on work to date. It would take further the question of credibility in a consideration of the magical series of coincidences which redeem the opening horrors and ensure a 'happy ending'. It would also take further the question of racial stereotyping by examining care-fully what Alice Walker has written about the writer's need to avoid all contact with the fantasies which the oppressor seeks to impose on the oppressed. The work so far described would, I thought, put the students in a position from which they could engage in Celie's development, especially through her reading of Nettie's letters from Africa, and her relationship with Shug Avery. They might then test their own findings against Alice Walker's declared purposes in writing the novel.

This was the theory, but the best laid plans . . . . .

The first obstacle which I encountered when we began to study the novel was the students' overwhelming enthusiasm for it. A genuinely active critical reading was under some threat from their undiscriminating acceptance of the novel's 'excellence'. I decided therefore to adopt an oppositional stance of sorts, and to involve the students in questions and activities which would challenge their enthusiastic approval. I asked them to assess their relationships as readers to the novel. Have you been so overwhelmed by the novel that you feel that any negative criticism should be silenced? Are you a *spectator* reader who has no real empathy with the characters but has been dazzled by its popular success? Have you simply 'enjoyed' reading it, and feel that any questioning as to whether it may have reinforced your racial prejudices (if you have any) would destroy your enjoyment?

The students' responses to these questions put me on the spot. Why had I asked them, and didn't they all imply that I had some, as yet unexpressed, reservations about the novel? The subsequent negotiations took us into an area which, I suppose, I could describe as the tension between 'textual productivity' and 'ideology', or, to put it another way, the relationship between the creativity of a text and its paraphrasable content. I was reminded by several students that when I taught them for MEG Joint English Literature, I had introduced *Macbeth* with considerable enthusiasm, but had then expressed some severe reservations about the play's monarchical power structure and its treatment of women. Earlier in the 'A' Level course, they reminded me, I had enthused about *Hard Times*, but had also suggested that the novel might be read as a Southern, Metropolitan author's misleading vision of the Grimy North. We came to an agreement that it is possible to read a text, disagree with its paraphrasable content in many ways, and yet value it for its essential creativity, for the quality of authentically lived experience being recreated page by page.

At this point, I asked the students to read again Celie's first seven letters, and to paraphrase the contents. The results might be summarised as follows: her father's excessive sexual demands on her mother; her experience of incestuous child rape; her mother's death; the birth of her first baby and its murder; the birth of her second baby and its sale; her father's incestuous desires for her sister; her father's new wife upon whom he imposes his excessive sexuality; the unwelcome attentions of Mr. ——— who already has three children by his former wife who was killed by her lover; Nettie's pregnancy by Mr. ——— and her own onset of sterility; her first image of Shug Avery; and her eventual self-sacrifice in marriage to save her sister, Nettie. The letters also record a number of beatings suffered by Celie, one in particular by her father when she dresses herself up to distract his incestuous desires for her sister.

Clearly, this is a horrendous catalogue, and I asked the students to transpose the narrative details to their own place and time and to rewrite the opening as if it were happening to them. The results were fascinating. Each 'new' version ended in either suicide or patricide, and no one was prepared to imagine themselves capable of Celie's passive suffering and generous self-sacrifice. That opened a long perspective on Celie's development and her ultimate triumph. One student (female) stated quite categorically, and she was supported by everyone else, that she could not envisage herself arriving at Celie's position on page twenty-one:

> I don't say nothing. I think bout Nettie, dead. She fight, she run away. What good it do? I don't fight, I stay where I'm told. But I'm alive.

I then asked questions about the students' attitude to Celie. Without exception, they felt 'sorry' and 'angry'. I therefore questioned their 'liberalism', putting to them the model of 'Namibian socialism' where white suburbans hold Wine and Cheese Parties (subsistence level living) with collections for the starving in the Horn of Africa, or support Band Aid and Live Aid Concerts—I suggested that you can feel 'sorry' and 'angry' about others' conditions while getting legless or enjoying your favourite music or your favourite Alternative Comedians, or even . . . but one student had seen me coming, and interrupted to complete the suggestion . . . or even enjoying a good read about a particular black woman's degradation as part of an 'A' Level course which might lead to Higher Education and an affluent professional life-style. The point was accepted with a certain world-weariness—what can you do about a situation with which you may well fully emphathise, but which you cannot even geographically touch, let alone influence politically?

Risking a certain bathos, I brought the students specifically back to the text, and asked them to rewrite the first two paragraphs of letter 7:

> Dear God,
> I ast him to take me instead of Nettie while our new mammy sick. But he just ast me what I'm talking bout. I tell him I can fix myself up for him. I duck into my room and come out wearing horsehair, feathers, and a pair of our new mammy high heel shoes. He beat me for dressing trampy but he do it to me anyway.
> Mr. ——— come that evening. I'm in the bed crying. Nettie she finally see the light of day, clear. Our new mammy she see it too. She in her room crying. Nettie tend to first one, then the other. She so scared she she go out doors and vomit. But not out front where the two mens is.

I asked them to 'lush up' the paragraphs with suitable adjectives and adverbs. The task proved to be impossible. Any additions would falsify the original projection of Celie's consciousness of what is happening to her. This raised the question of the limitations which Alice Walker has imposed on herself by writing in rôle as a young, naive, uninformed black girl. How can Celie present the significance of her horrendous experience? How can its author? This led to us spending some time looking sideways at the opening of Thomas Keneally's *Schindler's Ark* (also set for Paper 2 of the syllabus), and his production of a lushly adjectivalised prose which almost disguises the genocidal history which Schindler passes by in his characteristically opulent fashion.[4] We then watched the 'Genocide' episode from ITV's *World at War* series, with its combination of horrific images of the Holocaust and the controlled sobriety of Laurence Olivier's delivery of the commentary.[5] This experience provided an unexpected bonus—an interview with Sir Anthony Eden (as he then was) reflecting on the House of Commons' awareness of the Holocaust. The students laughed in disbelief at his crass, terribly English understatement in which his vision of 'the dignity of the House' clearly displaces the horror of what was being perpetrated on real people. However, they were clearly very moved by the quiet but intensive recollections of survivors featured in the programme.

When we returned to *The Color Purple*, the students decided that Alice Walker had imposed the right discipline on her material—a careful understatement through a limited 'spoken' language written down of experienced horrors in letters to a correspondent who doesn't answer—and several students made an interesting connection between divine silence in *Genocide* and *The Color Purple*.

I decided that we should look further at Alice Walker's self-imposed discipline, and asked the students to consider what happens when an author chooses to operate in the first person and the narrator is not, like the author, a literate, well-informed consciousness, but an illiterate, uninformed, unaware, and deprived consciousness who can describe horrendous events which might drive some to suicide and others to murder, and who seems tragically unaware of her own potential for resisting the oppression to which she is subject. Where does such a writing strategy place you as a reader?

One student suggested that we become God because we are being addressed. Another pointed to the novel as a correspondence to which we relate as privileged eavesdroppers. A third student suggested that reading the opening had made her feel like a helpless spectator but that the novel's development had replaced such feelings with a strong sense of satisfaction that ultimately Celie triumphs. That observation prompted a number of students to conclude that their initial feelings of helplessness (and outrage) were stimulated by the novelist to engage them in reading the rest of the novel as an imaginative 'rescue act'. Perhaps, therefore, reading is not such a futile response to other peoples' oppressions.

At this point, I introduced the students to some comments by Alice Walker on the writing of the novel. She has let it be known, for instance, that the character of Celie is based on her great-grandmother who was raped at the age of twelve by her slave-master, and she wrote in *Newsweek* (21/7/82) that

I liberated her from her own history . . . I wanted her to be happy.

She has also written of the novel's ending:

Fortunately, I was able to bring Celie's own children back to her (a unique power of novelists).[6]

I asked the students whether there might be an element of wish-fulfilment in *The Color Purple*. Some thought that the novel did contain obviously contrived elements, none more so than the survival of Celie's children and the revelation that her father was not her father but her step-father.

This led us on to ask whether *The Color Purple* can be read, in some ways, as a Fairy Tale. Several students suggested parallels with *The Tempest* and other late Shakespearian plays—that which was lost is now found. Others detected parallels with the Ugly Duckling and Cinderella. Celie is very passive and long-suffering and her 'ugliness' is emphasised in the text. But they felt comfortable with this and suggested that such intertextual features were quite appropriate in a text which was in effect as much a rescue act of an oppressed character as many a fairy tale.

I then directed the students to an area suggested by previous discussions—Alice Walker's view of Fantasy—and asked them to consider the following statement:

> The duty of the writer is not to be tricked, seduced or goaded into verifying by imitation, or even rebuttal, other people's fantasies. In an oppressive society it may well be that *all* fantasies indulged in by the oppressor are destructive to the oppressed. To become involved in any way at all is, at the very least, to lose time defining yourself.[7]

I offered this as a way of confronting the students with a heavily qualified response to *The Color Purple* by the black feminist writer, Trudier Harris, who, while asserting for herself the absolute imperative of continuing to teach *The Color Purple*, questions the ways in which it has been received by white readers.[8] I put to the students the possibility that a racially prejudiced white reader might read the novel as an endorsement of his or her own fantasies about black people. The following insights might, for instance, be gained into black life: a. Black people have no sexual morality, and black men, in particular, see no limits on their sexual behaviour; b. The organisation of the family unit in black culture is very weak, if indeed it exists at all. Black people have oddly permanent relationships outside marriage. They are only too ready to break up marriages to create less formal but more sexually promiscuous arrangements; c. Black men abuse their women, usually by beating them, and if this doesn't work, they kill them; d. Black men abuse their children; they are either indifferent to their existence, or they rape them.

The students conceded that, put like that, the novel did seem to paint a damning picture of black life. Or did it? One student found support from the rest when she argued that the novel creates a *specific* experience and does not attempt to create black life in general. Celie is being rescued from a particular oppression, and she is a particular woman, not *the* Black Woman.

The problem remained, however, of Alice Walker's presentation of the men, and I reintroduced the subject of the Fairy Tale with this statement from Trudier Harris: describing her experience of teaching the novel:

> One student, older, married, and with a child of his own, told me after class one day that he couldn't read the book because of its portrayal of sexual abuse. When he finally got beyond his initial moral repugnance, he became the center of several discussions. His responses were especially important to me because he was the most articulate of the black males in the class. How Walker had presented them—or failed to present them, from his point of view—gave him several days of intellectual exercise.
>
> This student maintained that Walker had very deliberately deprived all the black male characters in the novel of any positive identity. From giving Albert

a blank instead of a name, to having the only supportive males be young and pot-heads or middle-aged and henpecked (as is the husband of Sophie's sister, for whom Celie makes a pair of pants and whose only goal in life seems to be to please his wife—because she can beat him up?), to giving Du Bois' last name a different spelling, this student thought black men had been stripped of their identities and thus their abilities to assume the roles of men. And consider the case of poor Harpo, who doesn't even realise when he has a good thing and loses it because he has such warped notions of manhood. No man in the novel is respectable, this student maintained, not even Albert (because he can only change in terms of doing things that are traditionally considered sissified, such as sewing and gossiping). And what about the good preacher who goes off to Africa, I asked him. He's not an exception either, the response came back, because he must get down on his knees and ask a woman for permission to get married. All the men, the student concluded, fit into that froglike perception Celie has of them. And the problem with frogs? None of them can turn into princes.[9]

Arguing against this detail (Albert's initial description as 'Mr. ———', for instance, is an effective way of presenting Celie's alienation from him), the students produced a general refutation which sounded what was becoming established as the Key-Note (They *had* just finished reading *Hard Times!*) of their response to the novel—*Color Purple* enacts an imaginative rescue not only of Celie but also of Albert and Harpo, which gradually reduces their over-bearing machismo and 'tames' them. To test the suggestion, I invited the students to pursue the development of these two characters through the novel. This reinforced the students' sense that they were engaging in a specific and *fictional* account and not a drama meant to be representative of black men in general. They conceded that Harpo's progress from the twelve-year-old thug who breaks Celie's scalp with a rock to the husband who gives Sofia unremitting support, and Albert's conversion to a born-again feminist who sews and gossips with Celie, are in some ways open to objection. After all, Albert's conversion *is* offered in activities which are traditionally 'feminine' and that could be seen as demeaning male and female. But the students saw the symmetrical planning of the two men's development as an essential supportive element in Alice Walker's symmetrical planning of Celie's rescue from the shattering of family relationships with which her fiction begins and her eventual placement at the centre of an extended family.

The ménage à trois (Celie, Albert, Shug) which forms the nucleus of Celie's extended family gave the students a problem. It seemed unfair that Albert should, after all, be allowed to continue his relationships with both women. Perhaps, they decided, it was not so much a question of what Albert does or does not deserve, but a dramatisation of Celie's strength and generosity. That point, they also decided, made the reunion with her children and her sister, based as it is on a series of improbable coincidences, acceptable as a dramatisation of what such strength and generosity deserves.

The place of Shug Avery in Celie's story presented the students with no problems. Obviously, Alice Walker presents the relationship at times in a verbally and physically very explicit manner but the students were at one in arguing that this is the one relationship in the novel which offers Celie the personal happiness denied to her, for one reason or another, in all other relationships until the end of the novel.

Clearly, the students were prepared to allow Alice Walker a great deal of latitude in the technical dispositions of her novel. After all, she asks her readers to accept that the opening letters are being written by an illiterate young girl; that Celie's sister, Nettie, will run away and find herself bound for Africa with the couple who have adopted Celie's 'lost' children; that Albert will keep rather than destroy Nettie's letters to Celie; that there will be a reformation of the novel's men; that there will be a magical ending. For the students, technical contrivances were perfectly acceptable because of the overwhelming impact of Celie's 'voice', and that, I suggest, is a minor testimony to Alice Walker's technical triumph in creating the effect of an authentic personality detailing her various oppressions and her eventual triumphs.

The symmetry of Celie's development proved, for me, ultimately, non-negotiable territory:

> Well, you got me behind you, anyway, say Harpo. And I love every judgement you ever made. He move up and kiss her where her nose was stitch.
> Sofia toss her head. Everybody learn something in life, she say. And they laugh.[10]

The ironies of that quotation seemed to me, at first, a most appropriate comment on my experience in teaching *The Color Purple*, but, on reflection, Celie's comment on the possibility that she might finally be reunited with Shug seems more apposite:

> If she come, I be happy. If she don't, I be content. And then I figure this the lesson I was suppose to learn.[11]

Notes and References

1. Alice Walker, *The Color Purple*, The Women's Press, 1983—Winner of the Pulitzer Price for Fiction 1983; but see also Alice Walker, *In Search of Our Mothers' Gardens*, The Women's Press, 1984, especially 'If the Present Looks Like the Past, What Does the Future Look Like?' pp. 290–312, and 'Writing *The Color Purple*', pp. 355–360. To avoid confusion, I should add that the first article was titled 'Embracing the Dark and the Light' when it first appeared in *Essence* 13 (July 1982) and the second was titled '*The Color Purple* Didn't Come Easy' when it appeared in *San Francisco Chronicle Review*, 10, October 1982.
2. *The Color Purple* (USA/1986): Director Steven Spielberg; Technical Adviser

Alice Walker: Eleven Oscar nominations—none awarded; ironically *Out of Africa* won seven.

The course of study described here ended with a critical study of Spielberg's adaptation. I have not the space to deal with this element in detail, but the experience was most enlightening for the students. First, it clarified for them the chronology of the novel. It was also initially a dramatic tear-jerker. This, however, was a momentary aberration and they soon began to question Spielberg's product, discovering that where Alice Walker *controls* the most horrendous and most dramatic of her narrative materials, Spielberg *disguises* such matters as Celie's abuse and her relationship with Shug Avery by selective omission and *dilutes* their impact with a combination of lusciously coloured and artfully designed beautiful images complemented by a serene Hollywood musical score by Quincy Jones. We were all left wondering just how much say Alice Walker had had as technical adviser.

3. Trudier Harris, 'On *The Color Purple*, Stereotypes and Silence', *Black American Literature Forum*, 18, (Winter (1984), p. 156.
4. Thomas Keneally, *Schindler's Ark*, Hodder and Stoughton, 1982. The passages in question are from the 'Prologue Autumn 1943'.

In Poland's deepest autumn, a tall young man in an expensive overcoat, double-breasted dinner jacket beneath it and—in the lapel of the dinner jacket— a large ornamental gold-on-black enamel swastika, emerged from a fashionable apartment block in Straszewskiego Street on the edge of the ancient centre of Cracow, and saw his chauffeur waiting with fuming breath by the open door of an enormous and, even in this blackened world, lustrous Adler limousine . . . .

In the black leather interior of the Adler as it raced along the tramtracks in what was until recently the Jewish Ghetto, Herr Schindler chain smoked, as ever. But it was composed chain smoking. There was never tension in his hands; he was stylish. His manner implied that he knew where the next cigarette was coming from and the next bottle of cognac. Only he could have told us whether he had to succour himself from a flask as he passed by the mute, black village of Prokocim and saw, on the railway line to Lwów, a string of stalled cattle wagons, which might hold infantry or prisoners or even—though the odds on this were long—cattle. (pp. 13/17.)

5. 'Genocide', episode twenty of the television series, *World At War*, is available from video dealers at around £13.
6. Alice Walker, *In Search of Our Mothers' Gardens*, p. 359.
7. ibid, p. 312.
8. Trudier Harris, ibid, p. 155.
9. ibid, pp. 158/9.
10. *Color Purple*, p. 238.
11. ibid, p. 240.

See also:

Rainwater and Scheick, *Contemporary American Women Writers*, University Press of Kentucky, 1985, for 'The Dialect and Letters of *The Color Purple*' by Elizabeth Fifer, which includes a comprehensive bibliography up to and including 1982.

Bradbury and Ro, *Contemporary American Fiction*, Edward Arnold, 1987, for Robert B. Stepto, 'After the 1960's: The Boom in Afro-American Fiction'.

Susan Willis, *Specifying*, The University of Wisconsin Press, 1987, for an article on 'Alice Walker's Women'.

JOHN OSBORNE: ANGRY YOUNG WOMEN

David Walton

Not long ago I read *Look Back In Anger* with a group of seventeen year olds. For the sake of variety, it was decided that I (a middle aged male) should read Alison's part, while the roles of Jimmy and Cliff were read by two of the girls. Although discussions about sexual stereotyping, role reversal (in both real life and literature) are a feature of the English syllabus in earlier years, I have to confess that this particular exercise was not a planned attempt to cross the gender divide.

It took a little time to settle into the pattern of females responding to male cues and vice versa, but it also became slowly apparent that while the girls quite relished being Jimmy and Cliff, I was finding the part of Alison more and more frustrating. The girls enjoyed the longer speeches, wit, humour, boisterousness and generally more demanding nature of their roles, while I resented the supportive, subservient nature of mine.

An informal read-through being what it is, I grumbled a bit during Act One about how Alison was being treated. The girls nodded in agreement, and at the end of the Act we decided to have a more comprehensive investigation of how males and females are presented in the play. None of the girls volunteered to read Alison's part after this, although there was a demand for Helena's and others', and for the first time in several handlings of the play with Sixth Formers, I was noticing things that I hadn't before.

We decided to look at how the play portrays men and women, with the students (all females) working in pairs. We established the criteria we would work on (amount spoken; types of language used by males to or about females and vice versa; presentation of characters through dialogue or directions; activities undertaken etc). There was remarkable agreement in what the students came up with, although details varied, and I think it is worthwhile setting out what kind of picture emerged.

The play opens with Jimmy and Cliff lounging horizontally in armchairs, reading the Sunday papers. Alison is leaning over the ironing board, where she works for the next fifteen pages, until bowled over and injured by male playfulness. Not only does she iron for Jimmy, but for Cliff too. In an identical opening to the Third Act, Helena has taken over at the ironing board, and volunteers to wash Cliff's shirt. Such roles are unquestioned. In the previous Act, Alison has told Helena that it is wonderful to have another woman to help and Helena remarks that looking after one man is enough, 'but two is rather an undertaking'. The women cook, mend, wash, iron and skivvy. This selflessness is not simply taken for granted, it is also resented. Some of the girls did not see anything remarkable in this, others were fairly incensed. Jimmy has a tantrum because Alison's ironing interferes with a radio programme, later he tells Helena that he is sick of seeing her behind that 'damned ironing board', but instead of offering to help, orders her to get 'glammed up' instead. When Cliff announces that he's leaving, Jimmy forecasts the grisly fate of being gobbled up by some 'respectable little madam' from Pinner, who'll send him out to work 'clean as a new pin'.

Jimmy is garrulous (he has more to say than all the other characters combined) and male lines outnumber female by two to one, but perhaps even more striking is the way Alison is talked across or merely acts as a prompt for others' thoughts. Cliff tells Jimmy not to pester her 'she's busy', to which Jimmy retorts, 'she can talk, can't she?' He contradicts himself a page later when he responds to her plea for peace because she can't think: 'Can't think. She hasn't had a thought for years'. Cliff grabs her hand and starts to put her fingers in his mouth, commenting to Jimmy that she's a beautiful girl. In the same episode he puts a cigarette in her mouth and lights it, then soaps and bandages her burnt arm. None of these is an isolated incident. Alison's role is to be acted upon, to be ridiculed, ogled, vilified or taken for granted. Much of her conversation, particularly in the First Act, services the speech of others, providing cues or reminders, rather than allowing her to establish her own interests and topics. It was this aspect of things that first caught my attention, and it also provoked considerable anger and resentment from students.

Osborne's presentation of Alison is worth considering more widely. She is called various names to her face: girlie, lovely, little woman, beautiful, darling girl, Lady Pusillanimous, Judas, phlegm etc, in a way that no other character is. Cliff, who undoubtedly cares for her, feels free to grab, fondle and embrace her when he chooses. We are told that a species of lethargy 'like being warm in bed' permits this passivity, and also accounts for her subjugated personality.

She is cast in a helpless role by some of the language used. Jimmy poses as a 'chivalrous knight' who rescued her from her eight-bedroomed castle where Mummy had 'locked her up'. Mixing his historical metaphors slightly, Osborne allows Alison to describe herself as a 'hostage', captured by 'barbarian invaders' of the sword, furs, spiked helmet variety. Some of Osborne's language is incidentally revealing, with phrases such as 'hysterical girl', 'evil-minded little virgin', 'stupid bitch', 'evil High Priestess', 'cow', 'tart', and so on giving their unmistakable signals. Alison's role in the development of the plot is that of an inert victim. In an attempt to tell Helena why she married Jimmy, she claimed that there was no choice; even if not in love with her, he had 'made up his mind' to marry her. When Helena takes Alison to church, Jimmy demands to know why Alison is allowing Helena to have such influence over her. In the closing scene, Helena inadvertently summarises this role: 'she's done nothing, she's said nothing, none of it's her fault'.

Of course Alison's personality is recessive, or 'elusive' as the author terms it, but some of the girls felt that her self-effacement had been carried to excess. Her father says that, like him, she prefers to sit comfortably on the fence. She admits that pretending not to listen to Jimmy is a weapon, but it also suits her. However, we all agreed that the level of masochism attributed to her is unreasonably high. She agrees that she hasn't had a thought 'for years'. When Jimmy expresses surprise that she gets on with Webster, the only one of her friends 'worth tuppence', she meekly concurs; she apologises for disturbing a concert with her housework, and she abjectly begs Helena's forgiveness for returning to the flat in the last scene. She sometimes defines herself in Jimmy's terms, recalling when she was twenty one, 'I didn't know I was born as Jimmy says'. Towards the end of the play, Helena accuses her of sounding as though 'you were quoting him (Jimmy) all the time'.

A part of the masochistic portrayal is the continuous sense of guilt placed upon her. She feels she is held responsible for splitting Jimmy from his closest friend, Hugh, and driving the latter out of the country. Her pregnancy, far from being a natural fulfilment, is something else she fears will be held against her by Jimmy, who will suspect her motives and feel 'hoaxed'. She dreads the thought of him watching her grow 'bigger every day', and she wouldn't 'dare to look at him'. So she keeps quiet and prefers to leave the flat and suffer in silence. The girls certainly understood this sense of guilt, particularly the Asian ones who felt that it was a weapon still used more against girls than boys; it was a form of social-psychological control that was difficult to counteract.

Alison's breakdown at the end, where she fulfils Jimmy's curse in an intense expressionistic way, is memorable if surreal. She lost the child and felt 'stupid and ugly and ridiculous', but what dominated her thoughts 'in the fire', burning and craving death,

was that Jimmy had wanted this from her so that he could splash
about in her tears. She collapses at his feet to the words 'I'm in the
mud at last! I'm grovelling! I'm crawling!' Jimmy is magnanimously
almost stuck for words, but not for long—he pronounces an
infantile requiem for her suffering in 'mocking, tender irony'. It is
hard to find anything in the play which remotely justifies this. If
anyone should feel 'stupid and ugly and ridiculous' on the basis of
their recorded behaviour, it is Jimmy. The students did feel angry
about Alison. They readily conceded that there were women like
her and that Osborne probably was drawing from life, but they felt
that he was being selective, and actually (through the anti-hero,
Jimmy,) getting enjoyment out of her suffering and inadequacies.
They were quite ready to aknowledge other dimensions of the
character—her social background, the courage it took to leave it
and so on, but felt that her experiences, as a woman, were always
being subordinated.

The presentation of male sexual attitudes, partly through Jimmy,
and partly through other mechanisms of the play, is another important consideration. Jimmy reveals his support for promiscuity in a
typically intolerant way early on, whilst reading a newspaper letter
from a girl. He calls her a 'stupid bitch' for asking whether her
boyfriend will lose all respect for her if she gives him 'what he asks
for'. Cliff, in his turn, just wants to 'get at her'. Alison reminisces
to Cliff that Jimmy actually taunted her with her virginity and felt
deceived by her, as if an 'untouched woman' would defile him.
Cliff gets mixed up with all Jimmy's women, he has apparently had
so many. In a significant aside, Jimmy advises Cliff that 'Today's
meal is always different from yesterday's and the last woman isn't
the same as the one before'. Women are consumables, something
you get through, rather like the 'women and Draught Bass' that
Archie Rice is so addicted to in Osborne's next play, *The Enter-
tainer*.

They can also be sex objects. Jimmy admits to Alison that there's
hardly a moment when he's not 'watching and wanting' her. He
breaks into a sweat at the sight of her leaning over the ironing
board and wants to have sex immediately. Alison is a 'conventional
girl' and tells him he must wait until 'the proper time'. A few years
later, in *Inadmissible Evidence*, Osborne has the sex-obsessed Bill
Maitland put it all a bit more crudely: 'Look at that beautiful
bottom. Don't go much on her face. But the way her skirt stretches
over that little bum. You could stick a bus ticket in there . . . It's
a beauty'. Although the girls accepted the convention of these
attitudes being dramatised for the theatre or other media, they
were quite disturbed by the idea of such reality intruding into their
own lives. They felt that Jimmy epitomised the stereotype of male

sexual exploitation and that the play offered no critical comments or alternatives. They examined their own experiences of relationships with boys in this light and it was clear that a shadowy fear of such behaviour was generally present.

Helena, by contrast with Alison, is not so inhibited. Having been insulted by Jimmy, she slaps his face, kisses him passionately and pulls him down beside her. As he is so chauvinistic with Alison, one might expect him to have more respect for Helena, who, he admits, is a worthy opponent. However, he only sees things in confrontational terms and behaves with sublime arrogance. He believes that she loves him because it must mean something 'to lie with your victorious general in your arms', and with messianic hubris declares that she is either for him or against him. He promises to make such love 'to' (not with) her that she'll 'not care about anything else at all'. While he resorts to the encouragement of naive fantasies in direct dealings with Helena, he is coldly cynical about the real nature of their relationship when he talks to Cliff. He explains that he is willing to sacrifice Cliff to Helena because of 'something' he wants from her, something he knows she's incapable of giving. Cliff is worth 'half a dozen' Helenas, according to Jimmy, yet he is still willing to let a real friendship lapse so that he can make use of her as a mistress. Helena was slightly enigmatic after Alison. The students felt that she acted in a realistically passionate manner, although none of them could believe that she actually saw anything in Jimmy. Also her departure is not satisfactorily explained, and the consensus view was that she had been introduced to bolster Jimmy and humiliate Alison further.

Even more sinister than this sub-human utilitarianism are the rages that Jimmy falls into and the vicious verbal attacks on women which verge on physical abuse. The first attack appears to be a tantrum brought on by Alison's housework disturbing the radio. It rises from exaggeration to burlesque. He accuses Alison of jumping on the bed, as if 'stamping on someone's face', kicking the floor, clattering the curtains, sitting at the dressing table like a 'refined butcher', or a 'dirty old Arab sticking his fingers into some mess of lamb fat and gristle'. He thanks God that there aren't many women surgeons, because their 'primitive' hands would have 'your guts out in no time . . . Flip . . . Flop', and in a hypocritical crescendo, damns the 'eternal flaming racket of the female'.

Another attack a few pages later begins with Jimmy expressing his desire for Alison, but they are interrupted by a 'phone call from Helena. Jimmy starts, again in low key, by regretting his heterosexual drives. He rifles Alison's handbag in a fruitless search for any references to himself, attacks Alison's family for ignoring him and, on Alison's return launches into a horrifying malediction

over her. He hopes she will have a baby that will live long enough
to look human and die. He blames her, in blatantly sexual imagery,
for devouring him, like a python swallowing a rabbit, so that he is
smothered alive in her 'distended overfed tripes'. He has sunk to
the depths of woman hating in which he is blaming Alison for her
own sexuality as a butt for his own frustration. With stunning
hypocrisy he accuses her of being predatory. Without, perhaps,
understanding the full implications of all this, the students found
it offensive and distinctly uncomfortable. They certainly took it as
a form of violence against Alison in particular, and women in
general.

When Alison leaves for church, symbolically betraying Jimmy,
he hopes that she will come back because he wants to 'stand up'
in her tears and 'splash about in them' and sing: he's booking the
front seat for when she has to grovel. This is the sadistic counterpart
of Alison's masochism. A little earlier he has recited a doggerel
lyric in which his confused frustration comes across. He is at once
tired of heterosexuality, whoring etc, yet has also had enough of
'empty bed blues' and home wrecking. What does Jimmy want?
he wants Alison to respond to him on his terms, not hers. When
she doesn't, he lashes out at her, and through her, at 'all the women
of the world' for sucking the blood out of men and butchering
them. Alison is the prime target but women as a species are
continually under fire. The students were prepared to be as open-
minded as they could about Jimmy. They understood his family
background and how it had helped to mould him; they recognised
the social frustrations and the nature of his 'crusade'; they acknowledged his fierce loyalties and passionate, insecure character. In
many respects he was seen as an attractive, honest person. It was
impossible, however, to ignore his attitude towards women, once
it had caught their attention.

What about Osborne's portrayal of other women in the play; are
they different from Alison, do they reflect a wider reality of human
complexity or are they further limited visions of type and role?
They fall broadly into two categories, and are portrayed favourably
or unfavourably. The unfavourable category includes Alison's
mother and Jimmy's own mother. Alison's mother is referred
to as an unscrupulous, hypocritical, vindictive, scheming female
rhinoceros who wouldn't hesitate to 'cheat, lie, bully and blackmail'
to protect her daughter. Jimmy's mother is less forcefully, but no
less bitterly, drawn. She too is a bourgeois snob who nurses Jimmy's
father lovelessly and is obsessed at having married a failure; she
was 'all for being associated with minorities, provided they were
the smart, fashionable ones'.

In favour is Madeline, who is nearly old enough to be Jimmy's

mother, but has nevertheless, as his mistress, taught the impression-
able fourteen year old Jimmy all he ever needed to know; her myth
is so powerful that even when sitting on top of the bus with her,
he recalls, was like 'setting out with Ulysses'. Also there is Hugh's
mother, a pious soul who, like the other three, we only meet
indirectly. She is an ersatz mother figure for Jimmy, simple, sweet,
unworldly, unlearned yet delighting in the joy of others. She sets
Jimmy up with his market stall, cries tears of happiness over
Alison's photo and speaks words of 'pure gold'. She is a madonna,
apotheosised because of her unpretentious working class ways and
uncritical generosity.

Helena is somewhere between the bitches and the saints. When
we meet her, she is definitely of the former. She, like Alison's
mother, stands up to Jimmy's tirades, threatens to hit him and
gives as good as she gets. All this, so it seems, on account of her
strikingly improbable passion for him. It is part of the myth that
dominant males are irresistible, and all women need is a good
slapping down to reveal this, as well as their delight at such
treatment. She briefly becomes a sex symbol, fades to the house-
wifely drudge and, with equal improbability, removes herself from
the menage.

Osborne's women, in other words, are stereotypes. They may
be cleverly drawn, diverse stereotypes, but they are either objects
of hate, lust or veneration. Alison sums up, without irony, what
Jimmy wants in a woman: 'a kind of cross between a mother and
a Greek courtesan, henchwoman, a mixture of Cleopatra and
Boswell'. With this identi-kit for a perfect woman it is no wonder
that Jimmy is frustrated sexually, socially, intellectually and
emotionally. What Osborne has done is to place women into clearly
labelled specimen jars of fantasy: perfect mother; bitch mother-in-
law; experienced mistress; submissive housewife and so on. Helena
only succeeds in climbing out of one jar in order to slip into another.
There are no normal women, operating as complex characters with
the full and confusing range of motives; they are extremes, types.

Our consideration of the play was, needless to say, not confined
to the issues that we have mainly been dealing with here. The
students read critical commentaries, including material by John
Russell Taylor, Simon Trussler and Ronald Hayman.[1] We discussed the historical impact of the play on British theatre; the
conventional structure as a vehicle for the unconventional content;
postwar society and its outlook; the 'angry' young writers and so
on—in fact a range of background, ideas and themes similar to
that which I had been used to considering with previous groups of
students. I think it is fair to say that the accidental role reversals
in reading the text opened up new perspectives for us while not

removing the importance of other considerations. There was, in many ways, an enhancement of these, other considerations because the students felt so powerfully engaged with their own researches into gender issues, they treated other views and areas with more seriousness and active critical insight than I had expected. There was undoubtedly a shift in the pattern of things to discuss about the play. Other areas had to make way a bit, or, to confuse the metaphor, a subtle re-shading of the whole play took place. It is a great pity that there were no male students to give their opinions.

The students enjoyed the play and, like so many of us, recognised that as the years pass, it dates noticeably. They were surprised that gender issues had not surfaced before (either in my teaching experience or in print) and felt that this probably said something about the priorities of critics and teachers! I couldn't help but agree with them. *Look Back In Anger* is a regularly set 'A' level text. It carries a modern flavour, as do other works from the fifties and sixties, which should not be confused with progressive attitudes. Part of its presentation to students at least might deal with some of the points raised here.

References

John Russell Taylor, *Anger and After*, Methuen, 1962. (Reprinted paperback Edition, 1983) pp. 31–66.
Ronald Hayman, *John Osborne*, Heinemann, 1968.
Simon Trussler, *John Osborne*, Longmans, 1969.

EXAMINING THE READER'S RESPONSE

HELEN LEWIS

'A' level examinations have been the subject of much criticism over the past fifteen years or so, and in 1983 the Examination Boards published a common statement of aims and objectives in the hope that it would 'bring renewed clarity and direction to this important subject without inhibiting or confining the teaching in any way'. Here I want to examine the declared intentions of the Boards in the light of the perceptions of literature implicit in the examination questions set at 'A' level.

The aim of English Literature at 'A' level is 'to encourage an enjoyment and appreciation of English Literature based on an informed personal response and to extend this appreciation where it has already been acquired'. The following 'skills' are to be tested: knowledge and understanding of the set texts; candidates' sense of the past and tradition; expression; 'the ability to recognise and describe literary effects and to comment precisely on the use of language', and 'the capacity to make judgements of value'.[1] Whether the manner of the testing is the most appropriate method of achieving the Boards' stated aim I shall discuss later.

What emerges from the Examiners' Reports the following year (1984) is an apparently genuine desire for the expression of candidates' personal responses. The Oxford and Cambridge Board, for example, looks for a 'freshness of response' that might 'surprise or delight the reader' and 'lead to the perception of unexpected qualities in the work discussed'. Cambridge claim to mark up candidates 'who showed at least the beginnings of a personal response . . . even if that response was, in some cases, misconceived'. London examiners expect to find 'the most interesting and exciting writing' on the unseen practical criticism paper 'where a personal response is particularly looked for'. And Oxford desires above all 'evidence of a candidate's personal engagement with his reading, and of his active response—imaginative and critical—to the works he has studied'.

'Personal', 'active', 'imaginative'—these are key words. If a response is personal, it is individual; if it is active, it is a dynamic process, developing and changing; if it is imaginative, it is governed by the way a sentient, emotional being perceives and shapes his or

115

her world. Ultimately such a response offers not information about an objective text, but a human being, the reader. The function of the examination is not merely to test candidates' skills, but to assist in the education of committed readers.

Such a concept of response points to the work of such Reader Response theorists and teachers as Iser, Josipovici and Rosenblatt, all of whom start from the principle that it is a misapprehension of the function of a literary text to treat it as a repository of objective meaning. While texts certainly possess objective existence, the potentialities of imaginative literature can only be realised by the active participation of readers. 'Literary texts', according to Iser, 'initiate performances of meaning',[2] dynamic events which can never be duplicated. In this connection Rosenblatt draws a useful distinction between 'text' and 'poem': 'text' refers to the verbal symbols on the page, poem to the 'more or less organised imaginative experience' structured by the reader under the guidance of the text.[3] In effect every realisation of a text by a reader brings into being a new reality because it is a new imaginative experience, and any evaluation of a work of literature is not a discussion of the 'text' but of a reader's imaginative experience in relation to the text. It is evidence of that imaginative experience that the Boards seem to seek.

However, the overwhelming impression given by 'A' level examination papers is that to most Chief Examiners literature does not represent an experience for the reader but an objective entity to be discussed. Over 30% of all essay questions set by the English and Welsh Examination Boards in 1984—the year following the publication of the common statement—required candidates to discuss texts in the light of a critical judgement quoted or implied.

Now all critical views are the result of an individual's experience of a text. If students are asked to discuss critical views, it is the experience of another reader on which they are being asked to comment, not their own. Unless their experience of the text is similar, their attention may be deflected from their own reading of the text, which is the only way in which they can know it, on to ways in which the text can provide evidence for another reader's view. It is well nigh impossible to discuss another reader's experience as an experience unless one shares it, and so critical comments dealing, for example, with the perception of subject matter or literary effects, tend to imply that these are properties of the text rather than phenomena perceived as a result of the reader's transaction with it. If they are seen as properties of the text rather than as intrinsic elements of a reader's experience, it is easy to assume that they can be discussed as though they enjoyed an objective existence. So, all too commonly, texts are described, analysed and evaluated without reference to real readers' experiences.

In the following questions, for example, the area of the reader's experience is already mapped out.

'Loneliness is the real subject matter of all T. S. Eliot's poetry'. Discuss.
Oxford and Cambridge, 1984.

'At the heart of *Macbeth* is a debate about kingship'. Do you agree?
W.J.E.C., 1984.

Romeo and Juliet has been described as 'a very highly organised play about immaturity'. Discuss this statement as a description of the structure of the play and as a summary of its theme.
A.E.B., 1984.

If loneliness is the 'real' subject underlying T. S. Eliot's poetry, it is tempting to ask what the illusory ones might be. The assumption seems to be that 'loneliness' is a kind of deep structure underlying the experience of the poems, yet the search for such a motif may imply the bypassing of the student's real reading of the poetry. Similarly the W.J.E.C. question implies that a debate about kingship is the essence of *Macbeth*, the real subject or deep structure that provides the play's impetus. The danger of such an approach can be seen in the responses to the A.E.B. question: 'Too often candidates . . . launched into an all-purpose answer on immaturity'. The question implies that it is possible—and even desirable—to summarise a play's theme, a reductive exercise in itself, suggesting that drama offers explication of an idea rather than an experience. But once candidates move away from the vital consideration of the play as a dramatic experience, it is hardly surprising if the end result moves away from the play into the realm of broad abstraction. It is the supposed subject matter of a text that becomes important rather than the literary experience.

I am not rejecting discussion of theme in literature altogether. The danger seems to me the suggestion that there is an extractable subject matter in imaginative literature just as there is in transactional discourse. If students are encouraged to read literary texts as discourse, literature will be in danger of becoming to them, in Iser's terms, an item for consumption: once it has conveyed its message it will have fulfilled its usefulness.

Just as the area of experience of a work of literature is realised by the active participation of the reader, so are literary effects. 'The ability to recognise and describe literary effects' is one of the skills the examination is designed to test, but when we consider how these effects are created, the requirement that students 'comment precisely on the use of language' seems a little ironic. Literary effects cannot simply be 'recognised': they are dependent upon the perceptions of individual readers. Yet the assumption in the following questions is that they are objectively present in the text and it is the student's job to find them.

Critics sometimes refer to the vitality and optimism of *The Canterbury Tales*. To what extent do you find these qualities and how are they conveyed in the General Prologue and one of the set tales?

London, 1984.

T. S. Eliot described Marvell's poetry as having 'a tough reasonableness beneath the slight lyric grace'. How far do you find this an illuminating and helpful comment?

Cambridge, 1984.

'The vitality of Keats' writing is nowhere more evident than in the narrative poems, especially "The Eve of St. Agnes" and "The Fall of Hyperion"'. Look at the opening of either or both of these poems to demonstrate what you consider the particular quality of Keats' writing.

Cambridge, 1984.

The London question is obviously closed: students have no option but to find vitality and optimism in the Canterbury Tales whether or not these qualities form part of their experience of the text. Few who answered on Marvell apparently found Eliot's comment either illuminating or helpful, for the Report comments:

Few knew what lyric means. Even fewer can tangle with 'lyric grace'.
No-one that I saw even tried 'slight lyric grace',

at which point I began to wonder whether candidates were supposed to be discussing Eliot or Marvell. The rationale behind the Keats question is hard to fathom. Were the examiners merely checking that candidates had not ignored the narrative poems in favour of the Odes? It is on the slenderest of pretexts that students are given specific parts of poems where one anonymous critic has found evidence of the 'vitality' of Keats' language (whatever that is) to discover, if they can, another 'particular quality', presumably characteristic of Keats' writing elsewhere, which may or may not be evident in the poems cited.

Even when there is some indication that the personal response which the Boards hope to develop is of interest, examiners are curiously coy about asking for it directly, and tend instead to suggest that there is a kind of consensus on readers' responses to texts.

'The world of *Comus* is intensely appealing to our imagination, that of *Samson Agonistes* grimly repellent.' Discuss.

Oxford, 1984.

'"Upon Appleton House" appeals to the reader through its rich variety'. How far do you find this to be true?

J.M.B., 1984.

'Faustus' progress to destruction impresses us rather than gains our sympathy.' Discuss.

J.M.B., 1984.

Despite the fact that the use of the word 'appeal' in two of these questions implies that some personal encounter is assumed to have taken place between the reader and the text, they are not designed to elicit a real description of that encounter. Indeed, the Milton question can hardly be answered logically. There is no such thing as 'our' imagination: the imagination is the most personal of human faculties, that by which each individual perceives and interprets his/her world, and can by no means stand for a sort of communal vision.

In effect candidates are encouraged in such questions not to develop their own responses but to take on the viewpoint of a kind of composite reader. Possible difficulties they might encounter are indicated by the J.M.B. Examiners' Report:

> When some made their own response obvious it was disappointingly naive: 'How can one be impressed by a man who sells his soul to the devil?' One might reply, 'How can one not?'

However, the wording of the question is a possible hindrance to the expression of response, and in this case the unfortunate candidate, required to discuss someone else's reaction, may well have been searching for something on which to hang the word 'impressed'. It may well be that other people's responses to literature function only as intrusions in terms of the student's response.

Several of the foregoing questions are typical of the evaluative stance the examiners often require. One of the objectives of the examination is to test candidates' ability to make 'judgements of value', and it is important to realise the relationship between evaluation and readers' own responses. If the reader in reading is, to quote Rosenblatt, 'intent upon the pattern of sensations, emotions and concepts' that his or her transaction with the text evokes, and perceives 'a sense of an organised structure of perceptions and feelings',[4] any judgement will be an evaluation of that experience rather than an objective assessment of the text. Yet examination questions frequently ask candidates to evaluate texts in terms other than those of their own responses.

> 'The easy discourse of a formidable mind': discuss this comment on Bacon's essays.
>
> Oxford, 1984.

> Discuss the view that 'The Dead' is the finest story in *Dubliners*. Comparing it with other stories in *Dubliners* bring out the qualities you think might justify such a description.
>
> J.M.B., 1984.

> 'He had the finest ear of any English poet; he was also undoubtedly the stupidest; there was little about melancholia that he didn't know; there was little else that

he did.' From your reading of *A Choice of Tennyson's Verse* how much jus-
tification can you see for W. H. Auden's well known comment on Tennyson?
A.E.B., 1984.

'In *The Moonstone* Collins' narrative is full of ingenuity, but the emotions of his
men and women are very simple.' To what extent do you agree with either or
both of these judgements?
Cambridge, 1984.

The quotation on Bacon can hardly strike one as a particularly
scholarly comment, and to expect candidates to subject to rigorous
treatment statements which are not themselves the product of
rigorous scholarship is unreasonable. A.E.B. examiners complain
that in answering poetry questions candidates tend to be 'sound
on what but weak on how', but the Tennyson question, while
demanding an evaluation, does not focus on the process by which
an evaluation might be reached. The focus should be that of the
candidate's own experience: instead it is that of a widely read,
highly critical fellow poet. In effect the candidate is expected to
become a different reader for the duration of the examination.
Furthermore, Auden's style shows considerable rhetorical flourish,
and one wonders how much the temptation of beautifully balanced
phrases affected the expression of his judgement. Finally, it is
difficult to see which part of the quotation candidates are expected
to tackle in their allotted forty minutes: Tennyson's music, his
melancholia, his intelligence, or his range of subject matter.

The 'correct' evaluation is imposed upon J.M.B. candidates.
Even if they do not agree that 'The Dead' is the finest story in
Dubliners, they are required to stifle that response and hunt for
reasons to illustrate and justify others' judgements. It is not surprising that 'links between "The Dead" and other stories were
often unconvincing'. Such questions make the Examiners' denial
that candidates are expected to agree with any of the critical
comments given for discussion sound a little disingenuous, and
indeed the Cambridge Report makes clear that in practice 'judgements of value' can mean agreeing with the examiners:

> The better candidates were able to see that the two halves of the quotation
> amount to an appropriate response to the novel: that the plot is absorbing but
> the people are not!

More recent end-of-course questions show little change from
those quoted above. Some Boards provide a section of text for
candidates to use as a starting point for more open discussion, but
on the whole the impression given by examination papers is still
that literary texts have an objective fixed existence to be discovered
and evaluated. The general unavailability of texts during the examination supports this impression: response cannot be separated
from the act of reading, yet the system can in effect require

candidates to remember the imaginative experience of the literary work without access to the process which made it possible. Indeed, the *process* of response, which evolves in the moment-to-moment activity of reading, seems, so far as the set texts are concerned, comparatively unimportant: ultimately it is understanding of the text in terms of the question given (the Reports are insistent upon this point), that matters.

Only the end-of-course papers for the AEB Alternative Syllabus 660 (formerly 753) consistently demonstrate a recognition of the relationship between the reading process and the understanding of literature and an appreciation of the value of real readers' responses. Typical of the Chief Examiner's stance are the enthusiastic comments on candidates' 'outstandingly interesting' responses to Beckett's 'I Gave up before Birth':

> The emphasis on reading as process and the ability to convey the stages involved in the process made these answers fascinating to mark, exhibiting the very best in practical criticism.

> Report 1984

The following question on *King Lear* was designed in order 'to prevent students from merely producing a generalised, secondhand account of the theme':

> References to nature are made frequently during the course of the play. Discuss what the word means to any two or more characters in the play. You might like to bear in mind some of the following statements while you are considering your answer, but you do not need to restrict yourself to material on this list.
> (Several quotations from *King Lear* follow.)

> AEB Alternative Syllabus 753/2 1984

Unlike the thematic questions quoted earlier, the specific requirement here that candidates should link theme to characters' utterances, and hence to what actually happens dramatically, and the provision of quotations to act as pointers give the opportunity for candidates to 'attend to . . . the actual experiences the text signals' rather than to 'broad abstractions' of theme.[5] Results indicated 'at best probing and reflective analysis, growing out of particular statements and circumstances', and examiners approved of the way in which candidates 'tangled with the central and difficult areas of the play' (Report 1984, p. 84). In that word 'tangled' there is no suggestion of a desire for candidates to surface with a clear conclusion, but rather an appreciation of the ways in which they managed to get to grips with the experiences the text has to offer.

It is the personal encounter with the text that seems to be required, and so the Examiners are not afraid to ask directly for candidates' affective responses rather than to suggest to them that they should somehow accommodate other critics'.

> What do you find the most moving scene in the play [*King Lear*]? Outline what

you find moving about it, and analyse the means by which Shakespeare has brought about this response in you. You need not take the word 'scene' too literally; a section of a long scene would be an acceptable choice.

AEB Alternative Syllabus 753/2 1984

Having been assured in this question of the importance of their own emotional participation in the realisation of the work of art, students are asked to analyse their transaction with the text. Implicit in the question is the recognition that any evaluation must be of an experience rather than of the text as an objective entity. According to the Examiner's Report 'the question, when answered honestly by candidates, produced personal response deeply rooted in textual study', surely evidence of the 'inner possession' that Dixon and Brown[6] see as the goal of reading at this level.

Any consideration of reader's responses to literature must take into account the ways in which students are allowed to express that response, and some Alternative Syllabi are developing alternatives to the literary critical essay in coursework. However, the discursive essay and end-of-course examination, with or without access to texts, are likely to be with us for many years yet, and unless the conventional syllabi allow for the development of methods of assessment that encourage the expression of real responses, many teachers will either continue to teach in spite of the examination, or deliver the kind of teaching described by Barnes and Barnes in which students become 'willing collaborators' in a process that encourages them to 'surrender their autonomy as readers'.[7] The basis for reform in the way in which English Literature is examined exists at present in the avowed intentions of the Boards as well as in the existence of appropriate models of literary theory and the example of AEB Syllabus 660. It would be heartening indeed to see the Boards' appreciation of active, imaginative and personal reading matched by evidence of a real practical understanding of the implications of the reading process.

References

1. The GCE Examining Boards, 1983, *Common Cores at 'A' Level.*
2. Iser, Wolfgang, 1978, *The Act of Reading: A Theory of Aesthetic Response* (Johns Hopkins, Baltimore), p. 27.
3. Rosenblatt, Louise, 1937, *Literature as Exploration* (Appleton-Century-Crofts, New York), p. 33.
4. Ibid., p. 33.
5. Rosenblatt, Louise, 1978, *The Reader, the Text, the Poem: the Transactional Theory of the Literary Work* (Southern Illinois U.P., Carbondale), p. 28.
6. Dixon, J., Brown, J., 1984, *Responses to Literature—What is being Assessed?* (School Curriculum Development Committee, London), p. 9.
7. Barnes, D. R., Barnes, D. & others, 1984, *Versions of English* (Heinemann, London), p. 395.

BEYOND THE CRITICAL ESSAY: 'A' LEVEL ENGLISH AS A COURSE IN WRITING

Andrew Spicer

A number of recent discussions of 'A' level teaching[1] have pointed out the limitations of the present dominant model of classroom practice which, tied to a narrow examining base, mirrors university seminars grooming students in the appreciation of 'Great Works'. Not only is this a highly distorted set of priorities—only one student in twenty-four goes on to read English at University or Polytechnic—but the narrow specialisations of critical appreciation and the 'scholarly' essay offer a very restricted range of writing opportunities which causes a severe discontinuity with the more varied practices operating in earlier years. The gap has widened with the introduction of GCSE Literature syllabuses offering 100% coursework and showing a less canonical approach to what constitutes acceptable texts and ways of reading and writing about them. The official guide to GCSE English contains a descriptive list of some eighteen ways of responding to literary texts other than the 'scholarly' essay, a list which does no more than document current practice.[2]

In a major investigation of 'A' Level Literature teaching—*Responses to literature—what is being assessed*[3]—John Dixon and John Brown are surely right when they argue that, '. . . the standard literature syllabus proposes a course in reading; equally—but tacitly—it demands a course in writing'.[4] They envisage such a course as encouraging the need for tentative, exploratory writing which is part of an ongoing dialogue between students and their teachers:

> This is a view of writing as process that runs against the grain of the usual model—the published critic—even though it is familiar in writers' letters and journals, or in another way in successive drafts of imaginative works themselves. Indeed, the idea of drafting, knowing that there will be scope for further reflection and revision, seems implicit in some of the best evidence so far; should it not be central to a writing course?[5]

Such a 'writing course' ought to build upon rather than ignore the writing practices students have attempted on their GCSE course. Whilst it is easier to do this on part coursework 'A' levels[6] which encourage more diverse writing tasks that depart from the critical essay and where students can submit draft versions along with their finished pieces, I am suggesting that whatever the requirements of their course all 'A' level students (in any discipline) need to be conscious of 'writing as a process'. Though my focus is on some ways—I am very conscious there are many others—in which this course in writing might be organised, I also hope to show what Dixon and Brown imply, that these cannot be seen in isolation from strategies of critical reading applied to a range of texts and incorporated in teaching methods which seek to give active learning roles (i.e. those where they are not simply receiving information but exploring and broadening their own senses of themselves as writers and readers) to students and which take some account of recent developments in critical theory.

A first step was to follow the suggestion of David Jackson and issue all students with a journal: '. . . in which to jot down fleeting impressions, to comment on how different areas of work are received, to write personally, to assess their own work . . . and to puzzle out their first responses'.[7] Students are asked to regard these journals as semi-private diaries to which their teacher has access but sections of which can be clearly marked as completely private. Where possible I haven't taken the journals home but read sections with the student present so that the writing is clearly and visibly seen as being part of a dialogue with the texts they are studying, with themselves and with me. Removed from the pressure of always writing for assessment, writing informally in their journals has often had a therapeutic function for my students, unlocking doubts, misgivings and problems which might otherwise have lain hidden and continued to form unrecognised blocks in their response. These achievements, grounded as they are in a complex set of specific personal and local factors, are difficult to document[8] and, especially in highly selective quotation, are apt to sound somewhat precious, but I shall risk an example from Vicky's journal where she is writing about her first encounter with Hemingway:

> After reading these stories the first thing I noticed is that there is a lot of dialogue. It's as though Hemingway uses the passages in between as links, writing as little information as possible. He also tends to focus the story around one or two particular characters, e.g. the man in *A Day's Wait, Manual, Zurito and the Bull.*
>
> I found *The Undefeated* was a bit too long. It became tedious when Manuel talks to Retano about Bull Fighting. The Spanish words didn't help much although I know they are necessary. I didn't know what half of them meant until I'd read quite a bit of the story.
>
> When the characters do converse they don't say much. A sentence at the most. The story *Old Man at the Bridge* is a bit like a Harold Pinter play with narrative.

Each story seems to circle round one particular theme, e.g. the boy's illness in *A Day's Wait* and the old man's animals in *Old Man at the Bridge*. (December 1984).

Released from having to carefully structure her writing, to sound certain and authoritative, Vicky has honestly recorded her doubts, hesitancies, puzzlement and interest in this distinctive author, trying to make links with her previous reading ('a bit like a Harold Pinter play with narrative') as she pushes towards what she feels is important in the stories: what isn't stated, made explicit, what surrounds the clipped dialogue, the spare, laconic descriptions. Reading this entry and those of others in the group helped me to understand what we might focus on in the lessons.

Over the two year course Vicky filled eight exercise books and her entries evolve from confessional narratives towards more abstract forms. Many of her later entries don't show the same need to verbalise everything in the writing but become sketch plans, diagrams of a story's purpose:

Dervla Murphy (in *A Place Apart*) has a specific aim— to look at the lives of people underneath the surface. More of a social document than a travel book. (March 1986).

This approach is best exemplified in Vicky's plan for the most demanding writing task required by this course: the 3,000 word extended essay. See diagram on page 126.

With such plans/diagrams it becomes easier and less threatening than with a full draft for a teacher to intervene through, for instance, suggesting further issues to be considered, probable blind alleys, qualifications or modifications to be taken into account, possible ways of organising and ordering the insights which have been reached. In this example (the title was Vicky's own choice), I suggested that perhaps her sense of 'individual aspiration' was a little simplified. What did Jude and Tess aspire too? Why did they have these aspirations and weren't they *formed* by social pressures? We discussed how some of her sections could be brought together (how Custom and Tradition might be seen as a class based order) and what kinds of secondary reading, given the emphases of her approach, she might attempt. This is a sophisticated example of the best work of an able student (who could cope with going away to read Raymond Williams); but my contention is that with any student this is the moment (after an initial plan) when intervention is most productive: when students have a firm sense of writing as a process of reorganising successive drafts, a process which is common to them and professional authors.

In the attempt to build upon the growing confidence in their own voices—which the journals encourage—lessons need to be

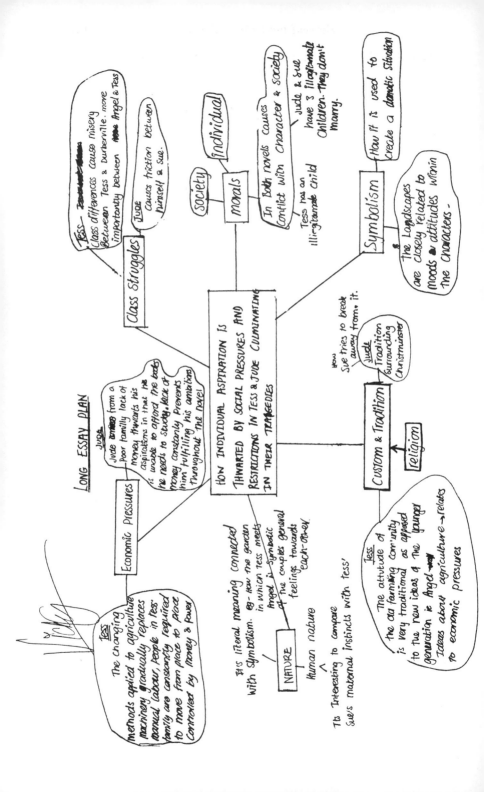

Long Essay Plan

Class Struggles

Tess
Class differences cause misery between Tess & D'urberville. more importantly between Angel & Tess

Jude
Causes friction between himself & Sue

Morals
- Society
- Individual

In both novels causes conflict with character & society

Tess has an illegitimate child

Jude & Sue have 3 illegitimate children. They don't marry.

Symbolism
How it is used to create a dramatic situation

The landscapes are closely related to moods & attitudes within the characters -

Economic Pressures

Jude
Jude comes from a poor family lack of money thwarts his aspirations in that he is unable to afford the books he needs to study. lack of money constantly prevents him fulfilling his ambitions throughout the novel

Tess
The changing methods applied to agriculture gradually replaces machinery manual labour, people in Tess family are constantly required to move from place to place controlled by money & power

Central
HOW INDIVIDUAL ASPIRATION IS THWARTED BY SOCIAL PRESSURES AND RESTRICTIONS IN TESS & JUDE CULMINATING IN THEIR TRAGEDIES

Nature
It's literal meaning connected with symbolism. eg - how the garden in which Tess meets Angel is symbolic of the couples general feelings towards each-other.

Human nature

It's interesting to compare Sue's maternal instincts with Tess'

Custom & Tradition
[religion]

Jude
Tradition surrounding Christminster

How Sue tries to break away from it.

Tess
The attitude of the old farming community is very traditional as opposed to the new ideas of the younger generation ie Angel — relates ideas about agriculture → relates to economic pressures

organised so that these voices can be shared in collaborative enter-prises. Almost all our lessons begin from the exchange of initial encounters with texts recorded in their journals but some have been spent not in discussion but with the students writing in their journals to each other about problems the text seems to pose, often in the form of a list of questions which they felt needed to be addressed. This idea of 'writing partners' who read and con-structively comment on each other's work (including essay plans or initial drafts), should extend to teachers also writing to their own student partners. These sessions often generated an honesty and clarity of response which students would have found difficult to reproduce in class discussion. It removed the necessity for me to be the central focus.

On a more ambitious scale and to instance work whose eventual outcome was not in essay form, students were asked to work together to produce a booklet on *The Merchant of Venice* designed to introduce Shakespeare and this play to a fourth year group. We had discussed the play in detail and looked at two ILEA English Centre booklets on *Macbeth* and *Romeo and Juliet*.[9]

> This is one of Shakespeare's best known but not necessarily best-loved plays. It is well known because it is often a set text for examination. It is disliked by some because it is full of unresolved issues.
>
> What follows is a collection of thoughts, ideas and opinions about the play together with some background materials and things for you to do. They are here to make you think and sort out in your own minds what you feel about the play and the characters in it.

Thus run the opening paragraphs of their introduction to the booklet, which contains collections of quotations, a web diagram of the play's themes, a flow diagram of the plot, a character chart showing relationships coupled with character sketches (a huge head with thought bubbles coming out surrounded by some comments on that character), director's notes on one section of a scene, some contextual materials on Shakespeare's life and his theatre, on the Elizabethan class system and the attitudes of Protestantism, discussion of the play's racism and role play notes for a different trial of Shylock. The stimulus of writing for a younger audience helped the group clarify their own thinking about the play in the course of devising these approaches and they tried out draft ver-sions of some parts of the booket with my fourth year group in another kind of exchange, another partnership.

As Dixon and Brown argue, students gain confidence as writers if texts are not always presented as finished products but as processes where the final version is seen as the outcome of a complex set of notes, plans, outlines, false starts and draft attempts, whose contradictions often remain unresolved.[10] Space permits discussion of only a single example: *Our Mutual Friend.*

As a framework in which to undertake the daunting task of reading a novel of nearly 900 pages my students were asked to make a reading log using the division of the novel into its original twenty monthly instalments as 'staging posts'. After reading each of these sections, they recorded what seemed to have emerged as significant issues, characters or plot lines and tried to anticipate how these might be developed in the next section. What these logs showed was both a fascinating and revealing account of the reading process—unlike so much writing about literature these logs were not retrospective accounts—and insights into how Dickens must have worked as a *serial* novelist striving to reconcile the dual focus of an overall design with the necessity of leading each instalment to a climax. To examine this process in more detail we looked at some sections from *Dickens at Work.* [11] Although this study doesn't deal in detail with *Our Mutual Friend* we could extrapolate from other examples Dickens's problems as a writer of serial fiction: juggling with characters' names and their major attributes, making false starts and hesitating over the order of events, struggling to package his material within the pre-fashioned instalment mould. We compared his techniques with modern examples from television series or soap operas where this process is now at work and we discussed what kinds of relationship serial fiction creates with its readership.

By disrupting the certainty and finality of the published version the 'authority' of the text and its author were called into question, opened up for debate and contestation in a way that students found liberating. [12] They became more prepared to read 'against the grain' and to question the ways in which Dickens had represented the working class including how the novel elides or occludes certain potential narratives in order to press forward to the supposedly inevitable and 'right' conclusion of secure and stable bourgeois marital bliss. They were also provided with a range of interpretations of the novel from published critics: we looked at extracts from Humphry House, Raymond Williams, John Carey and Stephen Connor. [13] These juxtapositions made it obvious that Dickens was the site of a critical debate in which professional critics had their versions of what 'he' and this novel were doing and of the relationship between imaginative fiction and its cultural context. Criticism's 'authority' needs to be opened up in this way so that students realise that no one interpretation is definitive, and that there is more at stake than simply a 'personal response', that interpretation is value-laden and political.

Having explored Dickens' hesitations and the contesting voices of professional critics I wanted to give my students writing tasks which could disrupt the novel further. They attempted one of three possibilities from the GCSE list: 'Write ons'—alternative endings/ what happened to characters ten years on etc'; 'character diaries'; 'Reconstructions' from the perspectives of minor characters. Unfortunately I can't document these materials—they didn't end up as coursework pieces because *Our Mutual Friend* is an 'exam text'—so instead I should like to offer extracts from Kate's piece on *The Spire* where she is writing the diary of a marginalised minor character, Goody Pangall, who is caught in the classic double bind of male desire as both angel and whore.

(from) *Part 1.*
What would he do if he found me dead? What would he say? Terrible thoughts I'm thinking . . . but interesting. My diary strewn across my body . . . he would read it . . . my dear husband! The thoughtless partnership. When he reads it, he'll claim I was insane. Lost my senses. And everyone will believe him . . . must believe him. The frightening thing is . . . I won't be able to deny it. I shall be dead, on the floor. Unable to deny . . . ever. He'll have triumphed . . . have an excuse. Any difficult questions, and he'll have perfect answers. They all will . . .

Part 5
A new fear has been set upon me. The very thought, and my body quivers . . . the Lord Dean . . . a good man, from what I know. A good man? . . . yes, I mustn't doubt this. He thinks he does good all the time . . . what is so wrong? . . . but knowing is more honest than thinking . . . The Lord Dean is strange and frightening. Yes, he frightens me . . . like no other. I'm frightened by his very presence . . . his manner. The way he walked towards me, and stopped . . . reassured me. So similar. So very similar to it all. A religious man . . . so there is no one. Nothing . . . no one to understand. Is this what they call loneliness?

I hope these extracts, taken from a remarkably sustained piece of some 850 words, illustrate the value of 'creative extension' at this level. It shows a sophisticated use of the diary form which demonstrates a keen understanding of the novel, revealing some of the silences and absences of this male text. Kate's piece seems to me an important stage in her definition of herself as a woman reader.

While I hope the last section indicated some 'alternative' ways of working with a classic text, students need the stimulus of reading a diversity of modes of writing if this 'course in writing' is to be successful. English departments might assemble their own materials but a conveniently available starting point is *Varieties of Writing* by John Brown and David Jackson.[14] Grouping their extracts into six sections—Autobiography, Travel Writing, Documentary, Letters, Journalism and Responses (critical writing)—this anthology 'attempts to bring together a broad range and variety of different genres and different ways of telling'.[15]

Though each section includes 'Ways of Working' which offer an imaginative range of 'non-prescriptive' suggestions of how to work with and write about the material, I think this book promises more than it actually delivers and should not be used on its own.[16] I asked my group to sample all of the sections but we actually worked in detail on Travel Writing, where I supplemented the anthology with a book-box which contained most of the texts from where the extracts were taken, together with other examples. I actually started from their existing opinions of the aims and purposes of Travel Writing and where it was to be found. Much of the writing consisted of superficial and overwritten descriptions of landscapes, the intention being either to sell or amuse. As we challenged this view through discussing the extracts and sharing individual reading, exploration of this genre seemed particularly valuable because of the light it cast on reading habits and prejudices about what constitutes the 'literary', about homogeneity of texts (*Letter to Iceland* incorporates a spectrum of different modalities of writing), and about how secure or meaningful the distinction is between non-fiction and fiction.[17] Their writing tasks included parodies of travel brochures, autobiographical sketches of childhood 'land-scapes' as well as analytical essays.

The government's abrupt rejection of the Higginson report's recommendation that the 'A' level curriculum should be broadened makes the task of widening the current narrow habits of 'A' level English Literature more urgent and I hope I have indicated how this might be achieved through more varied writing tasks, less reverential reading practices and the inclusion of a wider range of writing for study. The development of part course work syllabuses (particularly where teachers have the opportunity to get together to discuss approaches and examples of students' work in local consortia) has encouraged a greater diversity of pedagogic practice and choice of text. What I wish to suggest in conclusion is that there are limits to this progressivism. Recent developments in critical theory have not simply provided more readings of texts; some have also called into question the whole conceptual basis of the subject. What constitutes 'Literature' is seen as a central problem. *Who* defines, validates and privileges certain forms of writing over others? (In its present guise 'Literature' is a quite recent historical construction). What kinds of writing lose out, become hidden, by this process of selection? What is the force of *English* in the subject's title? Whose Englishness is it? Who is excluded? Isn't the fixation of Literature syllabuses with the single, autonomous text indefensible? Don't texts only have meanings in and through their relationships with other cultural products and with their specific social, political and historical contexts? I mention these issues not to deny what I have argued for in this piece (which has been concerned with method rather than theory) but to gesture towards that larger and more fundamental debate—usually referred to as the 'crisis' in English Studies—within which any practice at 'A' level must be situated.[18]

References

1. See, amongst others, John Dixon et al, *Education 16–19: The Role of English and Communication*, Macmillan, 1979; David Jackson, *Continuity in Secondary English*, Methuen, 1981; Kate Flint, 'A' Levels and University English Teaching—the need for intervention', *Red Letters*, 1982, No 12; Peter Traves, 'A better 'A' Level', *Eccentric Propositions* ed Jane Miller, Routledge 1984; Jane Ogborn, 'Teaching 'A' Level: A Two Year Plan', *The English Magazine*, Spring 1984, No 12; Roy Goddard 'Beyond the Literary Heritage: Meeting the Needs in English at 16–19', *English in Education*, Summer 1985, Vol 19, No 2; Nick Peim, 'Redefining 'A' Level', *The English Magazine*, Autumn 1986, No 17.
2. Margaret Maclure, *GCSE English—A Guide for Teachers*, SEC/Open University Press, 1986, p. 24.
3. 2 Vols, SCDC/NATE, 1984–85.
4. Vol 1, p. 59.
5. *ibid*, p. 72.
6. See the recent revised NATE publication *Alternatives in 'A' Level English* by Bill Greenwell.
7. *Continuity in Secondary English*, op cit, p. 206.
8. A much fuller discussion of this approach appears in the NATE pamphlet *Responding in Writing: The use of exploratory writing in the Literature Classroom*, Sue Hackman, 1987.
9. Paul Ashton and Andrew Bethell, 1981; Chris Dee, Lydia Kwiatkowska and Irene Shaw, 1978.
10. The facsimile and transcript edition of *the Waste Land*, ed Valerie Eliot, Faber, 1971, is an obvious example but such material isn't easy to come across.
11. John Butt and Kathleen Tillotson, Methuen, 1957. Chapter 1, 'Dickens as a Serial Novelist' is a helpful discussion, as is Norman Feltes, 'The Moment of *Pickwick*, on the Production of a Commodity Text', *Literature and History*, Autumn 1984, Vol 10, No 2.
12. Another possibility which I have used but haven't the space to discuss here is to use 'metafictional' works such as those of B. S. Johnson's which interrogate their own processes of composition within the text itself and which serve to reveal the norms of writing and reading which we have been habituated into accepting as natural. These texts encourage the use of parody which students often find enjoyable and which helps foster a detailed consideration of language and style.
13. *The Dickens World*, OUP, 1942; *The English Novel from Dickens to Lawrence*, Chatto, 1970; *The Violent Effigy*, Faber, 1973; *Charles Dickens*, Basil Blackwell, 1985.
14. Macmillan Education, 1984. I've also used examples of Popular Fiction such as spy novels or Cartland and Mills and Boon romances to allow students to discuss the workings of genre and formulaic writing and to look at the operation of the fiction industry.
15. *ibid*, pp. 1–2.
16. For a fuller analysis see Roger Leighton's review in *The English Magazine*, Spring 1985, No 14, p. 40.
17. I placed some extracts from H. M. Tomlinson's *The Sea and the Jungle* against Conrad's *Heart of Darkness* to illustrate this.
18. An attempt at a more radical 'A' level syllabus which tries to take account of

the questions raised in my conclusion is described in 'Challenging 'A' level', *The English Magazine*, Summer 1988, no. 20, pp. 30–34.

The above article is based on a version which appeared in 'About Writing', Autumn 1986, No 4, the Newsletter of the SCDC National Writing Project.

PRACTICAL CRITICISM EXAMINED

Roger Knight

Write a critical appreciation of the following two poems. You should pay attention to any differences and similarities in language, thought and feeling, saying what you take to be the main characteristics of each poem. (Cambridge, 1986)

Compare and contrast the following two poems by Norman MacCaig, who was born in Edinburgh in 1910. In addition to examining theme and imagery, you should also comment on tone and use of language, and any other features you consider to be of interest. (JMB 1986)

Write a critical appreciation of the following poem, paying attention to such matters as subject, form and style. (AEB 1986)

Write a critical appreciation of the following poem, making reference to its theme, its presentation, and your response to the poem as a whole (Welsh Joint Education Committee 1986)

Write a careful study of the poem printed below, paying regard to such matters as subject, style and total impression, and indicating whether you like it or not. (London: specimen question for examination 1989)[1]

Perenially, and predictably, examiners at all levels complain of candidates' inadequacies in the discussion of poetry. The exasperation is frequently palpable. We hear of candidates' 'unsureness of any critical mode in approaching poetry', of a widespread 'incapacity to attempt any literary-critical analysis', of 'a lack of familiarity with critical terms'—e.g. 'tone' and (in utmost exasperation) 'poem'! If such familiarity *is* displayed it is likely to be in a very crude guise: there is a proneness to 'listing figures of speech', 'to treat them as icing on the cake', to engage in 'irrelevant technical analysis'. This second set of comments comes from reports on 'A' level papers in 'Practical Criticism'. One could go on, easily. Let JMB examiners point to the general and, I repeat, perennial problem. They are reporting on candidates' attempts to write a 'critical evaluation' of Lionel Johnson's poem 'By the Statue of King Charles at Charing Cross'. The outcome was not on the whole very gratifying:

A central feature of this over-concern with the setting and tone of the poem was a remorseless listing of mechanical effects, often mis-spelt ('illiteration', 'assonace', 'metaphore') and rarely if ever evaluated. It was not enough to declare that there is alliteration in a particular line; there should be a reason for mentioning it, presumably the fact that it is about to be shown to contribute to (or even detract from?) the poet's intention at that stage, and some discussion

133

of its appropriateness is then offered. No credit is ever given for the mere recognition of figures of speech. Similarly, examiners reported that comment on verse-form often stopped short at counting the number of stanzas (usually accurately, though the additional conjecture that thirteen symbolised the unhappy King's fate is scarcely creditable) and the number of metrical feet (usually inaccurately—many were conditioned to write 'iambic pentameter' in the face of contrary evidence from sight and scansion), and, inevitably, the letter-labelling of lines. A second piece of advice, therefore, is to assume that the examiner accepts that the candidate needs not to state the obvious, and to come quickly to the point of what the poet has done with his thirteen stanzas, his iambic trimeters, his regularly-rhyming line pattern.

Now it will be clear from the selection of questions quoted at the head of this article that examiners will not always direct your attention to the same elements as the JMB selects. You may, across the GCE boards at 'A' level, be asked to attend to any of the following features of a poem: feeling, sense, meaning, verse, verse-forms, structure, style, thought. There is no doubt that examiners try to be helpful in this way. Most seem to assume, for instance, that the Oxford and Cambridge board's 'What is your response to the following poem?' is too open, too likely to provoke unstructured rhapsodising or ill-substantiated dismissal. On the other hand there are obvious problems of interpretation: the essential terms shift in meaning as one follows them across the boards. 'Language', for instance, tends to be used to indicate a discrete element by JMB and AEB, while Cambridge are far more likely to use it to embrace pretty well everything in that catalogue above. That, though, once a teacher has penetrated the particular board's code, is the lesser problem. Far more serious is the implicit view of the nature of reading to be found in the characteristic questions that candidates face. It is a view that becomes active in the styles of teaching it invites (and maybe necessitates) and indeed in the quality of reading on which it seems to insist. My view is that those questions advertise a conception of what happens when we read a poem that has implications beyond the Practical Criticism paper with which I am principally concerned. There is considerable evidence that this conception is powerfully influential in framing examiners' expectations at 'A' level more generally.

Clearly, those candidates who wrote about Lionel Johnson's poem fell miserably short of what the examiners hoped for. The 'challenge to discernment' that the exercise was designed to present was emphatically not well met. Why? The examiners don't tell us; they list the symptoms, not the causes of failure. For the causes I think we need to look carefully at what the candidates were asked to do. We need to determine the character of the poem and the demands it makes on the mature reader; and to ask to what degree the instructions candidates were given were likely to assist them in meeting those demands. My contention will be that the exercise (not just the specific poem) is inherently unsuitable for most of the people who do it, that the instructions tend to invite the banalities and desperate evasions perennially castigated by the JMB examiners; and that the general implications for the teaching of literature are too serious to be ignored.

Candidates were asked to 'write a critical evaluation of the following poem, referring to such matters as theme, feeling and tone, verse form and imagery':

Sombre and rich, the skies,
Great glooms, and starry plains;
Gently the night wind sighs;
Else a vast silence reigns.

5 The splendid silence clings
Around me: and around
The saddest of all Kings,
Crown'd and again discrown'd.

Comely and calm, he rides
10 Hard by his own Whitehall.
Only the night wind glides:
No crowds, nor rebels, brawl.

Gone, too, his Court: and yet,
The stars his courtiers are:
15 Stars in their stations set;
And every wandering star.

Alone he rides, alone,
The fair and fatal King:
Dark night is all his own,
20 That strange and solemn thing.

Which are more full of fate,
The stars or those sad eyes?
Which are more still and great:
Those brows, or the dark skies?

25 Although his whole heart yearn
In passionate tragedy,

Never was face so stern
With sweet austerity.

Vanquish'd in life, his death
30 By beauty made amends:
The passing of his breath
Won his defeated ends.
Brief life, and hapless? Nay:
Through death, life grew sublime.
35 *Speak after sentence?* Yea:
And to the end of time.

Armour'd he rides, his head
Bare to the stars of doom,
He triumphs now, the dead,
40 Beholding London's gloom.

Our wearier spirit faints,
Vex'd in the world's employ:
His soul was of the saints;
And art to him was joy.

45 King, tried in fires of woe!
Men hunger for thy grace:
And through the night I go,
Loving thy mournful face.

Yet, when the city sleeps,
50 When all the cries are still,
The stars and heavenly deeps
Work out a perfect will.

(The reader might like to 'answer' the set question before reading on!) What more would one want to say about this than that it deals in the currency of the most conventional 'poetic' sentiment, neither illuminating its ostensible subject nor doing justice to the supposed depth of feeling he inspires? The intensities of feeling supposedly provoked by the statue are present for us only to the extent that we find them in, say, the 'in memoriam' column of a local newspaper. But Johnson's poem is more pretentious than the comparison suggests. Lines 21–24 epitomise the qualities of the writing (not everything in the poem is as bad as those lines; but none of it is much better). The contrived melancholy of that stanza is quite successfully brought off in the way of such contrivances in all second-rate compositions. Johnson can, as it were, be heard sighing out the verse; it insists on a soft-centred reading and a soft-centred response. And it's quite empty. Those rhetorical questions are not genuinely pathetic; they don't give us a sharper sense of the sadness and anguish of the King's fate. The questions are rhetorical in the worst sense: there is no answer in them because there is no sense in them. They promote a conventionalised warmth of feeling suitable for *all* sad occasions. The very particular object is lost in the general wash of sentiment that the poem attempts to induce. And this of course is why it is such a bad poem: the title is highly specific; we have an exact location, a historical king and the writer in the immediacy of the first person. But in the event the closeness of attention we are led to expect is denied us: the loosely deployed diction ('rich' skies, 'passionate' tragedy, the 'splendid' silence that 'clings'); the heavy and ill-managed dependence on a degraded romantic currency ('stars in their stations set', 'stars of doom', 'art to him was joy'); the carelessly inconsistent presentation of the statue as both 'comely' and 'stern'; the wayside pulpiteering character of the final two lines; these are the elements of a piece of factitious versifying. Any sympathy we may have for Charles and any sense of the significance of his fate are spoken for before the poem begins; Johnson simply mines an existing seam represented by the standard vocabulary and rhetorical contrivances upon which he calls.

   How does one arrive at this kind of judgement? And how helpful is it to have such terms as 'theme, feeling and tone, verse form and imagery' in mind at the outset? First, it is surely the case that a capacity to speak intelligently about those elements will accompany rather than precede a 'critical evaluation'. *Must* accompany, rather; for it's a fact of normal critical reading that our ability to come alive to what we eventually distinguish as the tone or feeling is part of a comprehensive response that includes a sensitivity to those elements of a poem. Certainly the terms are useful, often indispensable, in discussion but only in so far as they enable us to bring to a finer point of articulation a response that is already there. They are points of reference in the formulation of that response; they are not separate entities calling for annotation and documentation. That is perhaps a commonplace. And yet it is ignored by the examiners in this case. On the one hand they throw up their hands at the common failure to venture a 'critical valuation' while on the other making it clear that you only earn the right to produce one if you have been through the preliminary hoops represented by the critical terms:

> The establishment of the poet's intention has been mentioned, and the purpose served by the effects he contrives. With the framework of the poem recognised, the purpose and effects noted for their significant contribution or deficiency, and the verse-form for its appropriateness, the way is open for the candidate to express a personal response to the poem, carefully weighing the evidence.

Criticism in cold-blood indeed! It's no wonder that they continue: 'Rarely, however, did this year's candidates find themselves able or willing to make such a personal valuation.' Surely we never build from an analysis of tone, imagery and the rest to a 'personal response'. The clear implication of the examiners' commentary is that we do. The consequences of such a radical misconception they see with wearied clarity; to their responsibility for this state of affairs they seem to be blind.

So, though the invitation to 'refer to such matters as . . .' is intended to facilitate a 'personal response' the perennial evidence is that it tends to achieve the reverse. The exercise is so difficult, the sense of exposure and vulnerability so intense, that those concepts selected by the examiners as helpful in the articulation of that response become for the candidates fragments to which they cling to prevent the descent into chaos. And really it is difficult to see how it could be otherwise for most of them. For is it not the case that unless readers have a sufficient depth of culture, enough experience in the reading of poetry, they may easily become victims of the apparatus offered? Now if it is to serve any purpose other than to compel candidates to make fools of themselves, an examination in practical criticism must give them the opportunity to draw upon a developed sensitivity to poetry—developed, that is, over an 'A' level course. But, as we see, the effect of the common rubric is to cramp teaching and to inhibit the growth of such sensitivity: the examiners' evidence is unambiguous; students are too often taught to 'evaluate' poetry through a process of labelling, standard labels provided. So what is the alternative? Let me say first that I think there really isn't one for the majority of students; that the usual 'A' level course probably cannot—certainly does not—produce the depth of culture necessary to make an examination in practical criticism a defensible option. However, such a summary conclusion will not make the exercise go away. How, other than through the standard apparatus might teachers lead their students to approach an unseen poem with more confidence? (The answer, I suspect, will be relevant to the approach to poetry in general.)

We might usefully start by asking what kind of questions we put to ourselves as adult readers when coming to Lionel Johnson's poem. They will not, I suggest, be for the most part consciously entertained; they will be embedded in our minds as a permanent part of our equipment as adult readers. Experienced readers will not be asking themselves about feeling and tone. Once one has established what, broadly, the poem is about (what the examiners mean by 'theme'), certain general considerations relevant to the handling of such subjects will enter into one's overall response. Though this will for the most part happen unconsciously, it is of course the teacher's responsibility with inexperienced readers to bring such considerations to consciousness, in whatever way he or she chooses. If I say that the outline of a critical approach suggested in the following quotations seems to me useful in approaching Lionel Johnson's poem it isn't because I think sixth formers need be introduced to such formulations. Rather, that the discussion of poetry in general will benefit from the teacher's contribution being informed by their suggestive power. (They are not, of course, the only ones that one might adduce to raise the appropriate questions.)

> . . . we may ask two questions. Is the situation so given concrete enough, near enough to us, and coherent enough to justify the vigorous emotional response invited from us? And is it, in its concreteness, nearness and coherence so far as they go, of the kind to which this response is appropriate?
>
> (I. A. Richards, *Practical Criticism*)
>
> . . . the author's defect of sensibility is a defect of intelligence . . . What we diagnose in expression as inadequacy in the use of words goes back to an inadequacy behind the words, an inadequacy of experience; a failure of something that should have pressed upon them and controlled them to sharp significance.
>
> (F. R. Leavis, reviewing *The Literary Mind*)

If a reader approaches 'By the Statue of King Charles' having been shown the value of Richards' concepts in evaluating certain kinds of poetry; if the teacher has been able to demonstrate, negatively and positively, the pertinence of Leavis's phrases to a great deal of writing in any age, but particularly in our own, then the student is more likely to be able to ask the relevant questions of Johnson's poem than he or she is under the imposition of the characteristic rubric (a rubric, it is now clear, that promotes a destructive teaching *method* when it is ostensibly intended to suggest the broad intellectual basis for it). Specifically, the student is likely to see that the poem indeed lacks 'coherence', 'nearness' and 'concreteness', that at the least there is no evidence of a genuine experience 'pressing' upon the words and controlling them to 'sharp significance'.

Richards' and Leavis's words spring from a subtler and more useful understanding of what should happen if we are reading critically than the terms of examiners' rubrics commonly reflect or encourage. (Though, ironically, the advocacy of those terms is a direct outcome of Richards' own handy guide to reading a poem in *Practical Criticism*—via sense, tone, feeling and intention.) It would be pleasant to be able to conclude that if the instructions were more carefully formulated, then the grounds of the examiners' complaints would dissolve. But even if (as I think should happen) the practical criticism paper as such were abandoned, that would not put paid to inadequate ideas about the nature of response to poetry. For such ideas are encouraged elsewhere by the examiners themselves. This is perhaps the most disquieting aspect of the matter: that the mechanical approaches so castigated by the examiners and that we see to be a consequence of their own bad advice to candidates, are actually *recommended* in places where one would hope least of all to find them. It might seem from what I have been saying that it is the terms through which candidates are asked to consider a text that constrain them; and that, invited to supply something as liberally defined as 'a critical appreciation' they would recover their wings. Unfortunately there is a good deal of evidence that what examiners expect in a critical appreciation is uncomfortably close to the enumeration of the surface elements of a poem that the terms used in the 'practical criticism' rubric provoke. What were the Cambridge examiners expecting when they asked candidates to produce 'a critical appreciation' of an extract from Coleridge's poem 'The Nightingale' (not in a practical criticism paper; Coleridge was a set author)?

> 'Tis the merry Nightingale
> That crowds, and hurries, and precipitates
> With fast thick warble his delicious notes,
> As he were fearful, that an April night
> Would be too short for him to utter forth
> His love-chant, and disburthen his full soul
> Of all its music! And I know a grove
> Of large extent, hard by a castle huge
> Which the great lord inhabits not: and so
> This grove is wild with tangling underwood,
> And the trim walks are broken up, and grass,
> Thin grass and king-cups grow within the paths.
> But never elsewhere in one place I knew
> So many Nightingales: and far and near
> In wood and thicket over the wide grove
> They answer and provoke each other's songs—
> With skirmish and capricious passagings,
> And murmurs musical and swift jug jug
> And one low piping sound more sweet than all—
> Stirring the air with such an harmony,
> That should you close your eyes, you might almost
> Forget it was not day!

Now, if I am right, this magnificent passage is as much about the power of Coleridge's imagination as it is about nightingales. The wonder of the poem is that it displays an intense and sustained sensitivity to the physical, the sensuous immediacy of the actual nightingales, whilst giving us entry to a country of the imagination purely. The harmony stirred is more than musical. Contemplating the profusion and luxuriance of sound Coleridge moves us, in the act of recreation, to a perception of the unity of the physical and mental worlds. (That we are in an imaginative rather than merely 'actual' world is surely indicated by the words 'And I know a grove . . . lord inhabits not', with their associations of myth and folk-tale). Any 'appreciation' would have to indicate some such under-standing. The examiners' comments, however, show all too clearly how far they were from demanding it. (It should be said in passing how extraordinarily helpful Cambridge are in issuing reports so generously documented with candidates' scripts and examiners' comments.) In asking for a 'critical appreciation' what they were seeking was an 'analytical appraisal'; and what, substantially, they meant by that is fairly indicated here.

> What should have been noted was Coleridge's account of the nightingale's song which he both suggests and imitates by his choice of words, his phrasing and by onomatopoeia. By his phrasing Coleridge imitates the short bursts of song which work up into a crescendo and to a long sustained note. The sound and sense echo each other throughout. The vocabulary with its combination of con-versational tone and poetic diction ('tis the merry nightingale', 'disburthen', 'inhabits not') its success in capturing the bird's song ('fast thick warble', 'with skirmish and capricious passagings', 'murmurs musical and swift jug jug') and with also its signs of addiction to the Romantic ('delicious', 'sweet') should also have been commented on in detail.

The examiners' specific comments on the scripts they reproduced strongly suggest that the favoured candidate is the one who is able to produce a pedestrian catalogue of such effects even though he or she shows no greater awareness of the nature of the poem; conversely, candidates who demonstrate such awareness will incur disapproval if they fail explicitly to note the effects the examiners list. Of one such candidate it is said that 'he writes an "appreciation" to some extent but not a "critical" one'. 'Critical' here clearly means analytical of the surface features of the poem; it is a narrow use of the word that can only encourage what elsewhere the Cambridge examiners have dismissed as 'irrelevant technical analy-sis'. In complaining that 'too many candidates resorted to a line-by-line commentary on "By the Statue of King Charles"' the JMB examiners said that such candidates 'failed to see the wood for the trees'. Unfortunately there is nothing in the Cambridge report to correct the strong implication of the passage quoted: that the same charge could be laid at the door, not, initially, of the Cambridge candidates but of their examiners.

Note

1. These rubrics are almost identical to those that appeared at the head of the

article on which this chapter is based (*English in Education*, Autumn 1983). It is a measure of the difficulties confronting teachers and pupils that there has since been no significant change either in the format of the practical criticism paper or in the complaints it provokes from the examiners.

TEACHING THE BEGINNINGS OF CRITICISM

DAVID WILLIAMSON

'Speak what we feel, not what we ought to say'

(King Lear)

My own 'A' level teacher objected very strongly, I remember, to our having to sit a paper in 'literary criticism', and he didn't spend much time in preparation for it. His view was that it was an 'unteachable' aspect of the subject, and he preferred the firmer ground of 'set books'. Also, to be fair, he felt that our experience of literature (not to say life) was so limited that we weren't in a position to make intelligent judgements on extracts from the great authors—we who had only just put 'O' level behind us, where all that was required was the memorisation of three slim classics. It was asking too much of us.

Few teachers these days, I fancy, would share those views. For one thing, we set more store by children's own responses to their reading lower down the school: whether we prefer class sets, or the individually-chosen 'reader', we will encourage pupils to express, however briefly and simply, their personal response to what they have read. And at GCSE level, the candidate who attains even Grade C is 'expected to have demonstrated competence in communicating an informed personal response to the texts studied' as well as 'recognising and appreciating specific ways in which writers have used language' and 'the significance of other ways' in which they 'have achieved their effects'. Gone for ever, it seems, are the days when sheer hard work and a good memory were guarantees of success. So it is not likely that an unseen 'criticism and appreciation' paper at 'A' level will be regarded as an anomaly, or the premature imposition of 'University-level' work on unfledged schoolchildren: like drama (and perhaps for some of the same reasons) 'practical criticism' is at present one of education's Good Things.

Even so, I sympathise with my old master's point of view, and agree with him that the difficulties in teaching this part of the course stem from the immaturity, inexperience and limited reading of our pupils. To state which would be otiose, if the essence of the 'practical criticism' lesson weren't communal exploration, and if (no paradox) the essence of reading weren't a personal response to the words on the page ('a judgement is personal or it is nothing', as Dr Leavis was fond of reminding us). How does the teacher avoid pontificating on the one hand—as his greater years and wider reading give him ample opportunity of doing—and, on the other, taking so rearward a seat that nobody learns anything? More would seem to depend on pedagogical tact and opportunism (not to say inspiration) in this 'subject' than in any other, with its complete absence of conveyable knowledge, or even a set of skills which can be learnt and then applied.

Of course there is a constant temptation to adopt one or both of these false solutions, not simply through inertia or desperation, but because of the need (for teacher and taught) to feel a sense of progress, of getting somewhere. It's a temptation to be resisted, none the less: we all know that pupils—and not just the least able— will grab at anapaests and alliterations as a drowning man at a straw, and shirk the difficult matter of responding to a poem by what one examining board aptly calls 'the Mrs Beeton-type approach, which lists by quantity the various stylistic ingredients, rhyme-schemes, caesura, enjambement, even punctuation' (London Board Examiners' Report, 1987). No, the sense of progress we need is that of a swimmer who, even though only messily dog-paddling, is at least keeping himself afloat. Our part initially, I'm sure, is to give our pupils just this confidence, to let them feel that, having the English language, they have all the equipment necessary to be a literary critic—what they need to do is to *use* it. (It goes without saying, I hope, that if they haven't the requisite intelligence and sensibility they won't be on the course in the first place. I realise this is a utopian assumption—but without it nothing profitable can be said).

For this reason, I like to start with prose, and reasonably modern prose, too. Not because I subscribe to the current cant about 'relevance' (all literature is grist to our mill, and in these days of photocopiers there is a superabundance of potential material), but because I think it's easier for the reader to recognise the voice of his language and attend to the thought—to exorcise the suspicion many new 'A' level pupils have that Literature is somehow esoteric by nature, another language, and they are embarked on unlocking its doors for Secret Meanings. The primacy of thought, the fact that the fellow is *telling* us something, is worth insisting on, I think, because (though a simplification) it's a truth that young readers so easily forget once they start worrying, as they have to, about how effects are achieved.

Nor is there any reason to stick to what is 'literature', strictly so called. I find a pair of passages (reproduced below) from J. H.

Walsh's anthology *Fields of Experience*—descriptions of a father and mother written by fourteen year olds—very useful at this early stage. They serve to remind us that all words that get into print have been uttered by human beings with an identifiable experience to convey, and that to recognise that experience and get a notion of the utterer is a part of what reading entails. Thus, the boy describing his father states explicitly his changed attitude to his 'former hero', Dad, but betrays more irritation, resentment and indignation (in a touch of sarcasm, for example) than perhaps he intends to. By contrast, the mother described in the companion-piece is obviously, for all the complaints, loved unaffectedly, and the humour which permeates the writing is evidence of a mind at ease with itself: the writer has no axe to grind. The sense of an author—or at least a mood—comes over plainly, and pupils readily see the difficulty of separating the described from the describer— see, in fact, that our experience of the description is really an experience of both.

It will be seen that one value of this elementary exercise is that it enables one to introduce some indispensable words in an easily identifiable context: attitude, feeling, intention, tone. One could begin, of course, with I. A. Richards' S.I.F.T. (sense, intention, feeling, tone); perhaps one will refer to it anyway; but surely it is better if the terms emerge 'naturally', out of the quest to do justice to a fairly simple piece of writing, and its easily imagined creator. The writer is nearer the surface, so to speak, than in most 'literature proper', but at the same time one needs to read between the lines. Descriptions of people and places provide an endless source of material to demonstrate how an artist's vision determines what he sees and conveys, and how the very words of the language militate against pure objectivity. To appreciate this even more immediately, the pupils might be asked to write their own 'neutral' and 'ten-dentious' descriptions of the same subject: the former, unless they confine themselves to mere sizes and colours, will be found well-nigh impossible.

It may seem a long step from this to appreciating the openings of (say) *Bleak House*, *Pride and Prejudice* or *Silas Marner*; but only by perceiving their respective attitudes and intentions will readers make much of any of these passages. Actually, they rep-resent increasingly difficult demands on the reader's perspicacity, for while both Dickens and Jane Austen invite to a simple 'placing' judgement at the end of their first 'movement', George Eliot requires a balance of sympathies throughout. Dickens makes his own connection between the London fog and the 'groping and floundering condition' of the 'High Court of Chancery', and pupils don't find it difficult to suggest why he should have begun his novel in this way—or used his famous idiosyncratic syntax. But the effect of the humour is less easy to define. Provisionally one will be content, I take it, if the exuberance of the writing, its variety, its rhythmic and accumulative power. are acknowledged: an individual, living voice comes over ι ιistakably.

Someone might raise the word 'satire', which (with 'irony') is an indispensable term—though quite a different thing in Jane Austen. I like to ask why she thought it necessary to write the final paragraph of Chapter One; with luck, its difference from what precedes will emerge without too much prompting, and hence an opportunity to ponder the distinction—surely so crucial to fiction—between 'showing' and 'telling'. Whether Mr Bennet is, like his wife, present for our 'placing', or pretty much the voice of the author, is a cognate question which can be pursued with some profit.

The opening of *Silas Marner* has nothing so crude (if thus we deem it) as the paragraph of Jane Austen just alluded to: George Eliot keeps herself well behind the words on the page. An obvious approach is to ask for the quotation of sentences in which the author is momentarily adopting the point of view of the country people, and to ask how ironical her tone is. The temptation for young readers is to see the passage as an attack on the narrowness and prejudice of the villagers, and an evocation of sympathy for the poor outcast weavers ('remnants of a disinherited race'). The discussion which leads to a less simple view of the author's intentions ought—if firmly related to the text—to be a valuable educative experience.

What of evaluation, that hardest of literary tasks, and hardest of all for the inexperienced reader? If one believes implicit evaluation to be an integral part of reading, not a later, and optional, exercise, one will wish to give a notion of criteria from the outset. This is surely best done as we seek to define the qualities of the writing before us, especially when pairs of passages are presented for comparison. I like to juxtapose Dickens' description of a London market in *Oliver Twist* with that by J. B. Priestley in *Petticoat Lane*. Dickens *makes* it, in his accumulation of detail, 'a stunning and bewildering scene'—we believe in it; whereas Priestley protests too much, and it is easy to quote bits in which he has got carried away: 'A fellow with razor strops to sell looked like a homicidal maniac. The sweat was streaming down his face, and one hand was bandaged and bloody . . . in a fury, he picked up the razor, and attacked a block of wood with it'. One will ask, then: 'Which description is the more convincing? Is there any evidence one way or the other?' And hopefully some other of Priestley's unrealities will be pointed out (as a foil to Dickens): the youth being '*jammed*' into an overcoat 'and compelled to buy it', and the 'little man, all nose and bowler hat' who 'was savagely cutting trousers to pieces with a carving knife'.

One can never be sure where discussion will lead, of course, and there's an art in deciding what issues might prove profitable. I wouldn't myself bring up the bad taste of 'all nose and bowler hat', but if someone mentioned it there's a comment to make. On the other hand, the question of cliché might be worth raising, and the relative merits of the following to be so designated: 'furious energy', 'dionysiac frenzy', 'dazed expression', 'eyes gleaming wildly'—as well as 'like a homicidal maniac', already quoted. If Priestley is defended (as he was to me the other day) as simply entertaining us by indulging in 'poetic licence' and 'humorous exaggeration', and not intending to be taken seriously—well, one is lucky enough to have occasion to discuss some very basic and important issues.

Actually, that notion of writing which sees 'liveliness' as a virtue irrespective of what is being said is so widespread nowadays that scarcely anyone is untouched by it. It is taken for granted in contemporary journalism, I suggest, and even finds advocates in schools and on examination boards (I am thinking of admirers of the prose of Dylan Thomas and Laurie Lee, for example). If one sees such 'liveliness' as merely boring exhibitionism one will not foist one's views on one's pupils. But what one values will naturally become manifest as the course proceeds; and as the class reads prose which has the virtues of reality and sincerity (in the many forms which are possible) pupils will be gaining the equipment to 'place' the shallow, the unreal, the flippant, the meretricious, the affected. Always there will be room for disagreement, of course, but I'd feel myself to be failing in my duty if I didn't sooner or later make plain my settled conviction that what one values in literature is what one values in life.

By the same token I believe that the language with which to talk about literature is the same as that needed to talk about life: 'literary' terms are mostly an obstruction. When reading poetry, one will need 'rhythm' and 'rhyme', 'metaphor' and 'simile'—but, really, how much else? The avoidance of 'technical' talk is, I think, one of the two necessary conditions for a fruitful approach; the other is an insistence that the poet is, basically, communicating something. The Romantic/Victorian assumption that poetry is akin to music and incantation refuses to die sixty-five years after 'Prufrock and Other Observations', and for this reason I like to begin with poems that have a decided 'point' to them: 'Aunts Watching Television', by John Pudney, is about the right level of difficulty, I find, but there is such an abundance of choice in modern anthologies that obtaining suitable material is never a problem.

Not that I concentrate, this time, on 'modern' poems: I like to introduce the question of imagery by reading the mediaeval carol 'I sing of a maiden', with its threefold pattern of similes:

> He came all so still
>> Where his mother was
> As dew in April
>> That falleth on the grass.

> He came all so still
>> Where his mother lay
> As dew in April
>> That falleth on the spray.

> He came all so still
>> To his mother's bower
> As dew in April
>> That falleth on the flower.

Is this merely a pretty pattern, one can ask, or is there an aptness of *thought*? Hopefully, the class will be led to see associations between the falling of the dew and the coming of Christ—and, more, feel something of the poet's wonder. Perhaps this is an extreme case of an image being necessary to convey the otherwise inexpressible—but to see imagery as integral to thought, rather than optional and decorative, is a step towards an appreciation of the supreme, Shakespearian, usage.

That metaphor and simile can be used merely to catch the eye, or disguise a lack of thought and coherence (not consciously, of course), is evidenced to my mind by the following stanza from Louis Macneice's 'Birmingham':

> On shining lines the trams like vast sarcophagi move
> Into the sky, plum after sunset, merging to duck's egg, barred with mauve
> Zeppelin clouds, and pentecost-like the cars' headlights bud
> Out from sideroads and the traffic signals, Creme-de-menthe or bull's blood,
> Tell one to stop, the engine gently breathing, or to go on
> To where like black pipes of organs in the frayed and fading zone
> Of the West the factory chimneys on sullen sentry will all night wait
> To call, in the harsh morning, sleep-stupid faces through the daily gate.

In asking why (for instance) the traffic lights are likened to 'Creme-de-menthe or bull's blood' one is likely to receive as many answers as there are members of the class. Are these views equally valid? The factory chimneys are like both organ-pipes and sentries—how is this possible? Why are the car-lights 'Pentecost-like'? Just as minds meet in 'I sing of a maiden', so they diverge with the centrifugal effect of Macneice's imagery, I find. (The legitimacy of each reader having his own interpretation of a poem—or part of a poem—is a question that will arise sooner or later. Who is to say what is correct? What does 'correct' mean? The literary criticism class is the place where these most fundamental of questions will arise).

One won't assume that 'Pentecost' is a part of everyone's cultural inheritance, and one has to be on the lookout for difficulties of this kind. The 'fall' in Herbert's 'Easter Wings' also needs preparatory explanation, though fortunately everyone has still heard of Adam and Eve. I find this poem useful to demonstrate the basic fact that poems 'do what they say' rather than 'talk about' things: everyone can see the expressive effect of the use of line, even if the rhythmical and alliterative qualities need some help in defining. Another useful short poem in this regard is Jonson's 'It is not growing like a tree'; here, the rhythmical contrast between

To fall a log at last, dry, bald, and sere

and

A lily of a day
Is fairer far in May

is easy to feel, and the final couplet rounds the poem off with a neat convincing finality: 'QED' is the effect.

Rhythm is surely a most important consideration: linked as it is with tone and feeling, it is the very breath of the poem's body, and no true reading is possible which is insensitive to its effects. For this reason I deprecate the teaching of scansion and metrical analysis at this stage: what have iambics and anapaests to do with real reading? Granted, the metres so described are the forms within which our poets have created, and *they* went to school to the metrists. But at a younger age, surely, so that by sixteen and seventeen the technical knowledge was utterly digested. Meeting this equipment for the first time in the sixth form, as diffident but maturing readers, no wonder pupils treat it as a key to unlock all poetical secrets.

No, rhythm needs to be *felt*, and the best words to describe it are those from 'real life': jaunty, yearning, flippant, foreboding, aggressive, jolly, peaceful, ecstatic, reverent. It's no easy matter. But once heard (and one of the teacher's main assets even at this level is his ability to read aloud) the effect of rhythm is surely palpable. Consider, for example:

Which two when they once meet,
The heart rears wings bold and bolder
And hurls for him, O half hurls earth for
Him off under his feet.

or

I have
That honourable grief lodg'd here which burns
Worse than tears drown.

'How does the movement *here* fit in with the meaning?' the teacher will ask. It may not be long before it emerges that the movement *is* the meaning ('poetry does what it says'), and the class's consideration of rhythm will have advanced far beyond what metrics can cope with.

There are plenty of 'primers' on the market which aim to 'teach' literary criticism, but surely it's best if the teacher selects his own material and deals with it in his own way. Only he knows what his pupils are capable of (and one can't make the opening lessons too easy, I contend); and in any case, this subject of all subjects is one that depends on the living interplay of ideas and responses. The pupils need to be able to buttonhole their teacher, to put him on the spot over fundamentals; and he, in turn, needs to follow profitable-looking sidetracks, bring along (say) a bit of prose from yesterday's newspaper to illustrate a point. Yet primers may have their use later on, when the pupils are more seasoned, and realise that a voice in print is no more infallible than that of their teacher. Another's chosen passages and juxtapositions are always interesting, too; 'why did the editor put these together?' is a standard opening question that can keep one going all lesson.

Written work for this part of the course will differ rather from that on 'set books'. Even when questions are 'open-ended' and demand an essay-length answer, the quality of the parts (I take it, for I'm not an examiner) will matter more than the organisation of the whole. Evidence will certainly need to be adduced: the ability to perceive key words, lines, sentences—to discriminate—will be a mark of the competent reader. But those who contribute well orally ought to do so in writing (a certain level of literacy being assumed). Here again, confidence is all-important: the pupil needs to feel that his own reaction is valuable and valid, and worth uttering honestly and directly. After all, it's the only reaction he can have.

Passages referred to

1. From *Fields of Experience*

My Father

When I was small, my 'Daddy' appeared to be the most learned and powerful man I knew. He and my mother were my protection against bullying and teasing. They were always at hand, and when I was near 'Daddy' I was safe.

Since then, my father's name has changed to a blunt 'Dad'. His significance in my life seems to have grown very small, and that kindliness and affection seems absent. He has narrowed down to a plain bread-winner, which I should be, and am, thankful for. In his sight, I seem to have ceased to develop socially and mentally. I am often opposed by Dad when I state a fact. I cannot be relied upon.

In my father's sight I am an unerudite simpleton, towered over by the infallible knowledge of a being who is in every way superior to me (the being, of course, being Dad). One example of the failure of this knowledge is here recorded.

One Sunday morning I rose early, ate a quick breakfast, and prepared myself for church, to which I cycle by myself each week. With very little time in hand, I began to look for my cycle-clips. I picked my way through the legs of dressing-gowned brothers, and searched on the floor. Then I approached Dad, who was wearing baggy trousers and maroon braces with his striped pyjama-top, his hair looking very unkempt and his fattish chin very stubbly. He was not wearing his glasses, and the bald patch on the top of his head was very noticeable. He was reading *The Observer*, and occasionally he took sips of tea from a cup which stood on the table.

'Dad', I said, 'are you sitting on my cycle-clips?'

'No', he answered, as if I was stupid.

'Oh, I just wondered.' And I searched elsewhere.

But the search was fruitless. I again enquired about the possibility, remote as it was, that Dad might be sitting on my trouser-clips.

'No, damn you!' Dad shouted, his temper becoming short. 'If I was sitting on your bloomin' cycle-clips I would tell you.'

Dad probably added a 'Blast' or another 'Damn you'; I cannot remember rightly. I almost gave up the search for my cycle-clips, and knew I would be late for church. A few minutes later Dad stood up to pour another cup of tea, and there, on Dad's chair, were my long-lost cycle-clips. Dad offered no apology, and when he saw that I was speaking as if I was annoyed, he referred to me as 'impertinent'. He felt that his dignity could suffer no opposition of any sort, and that is still Dad's main weakness.

My Mother

My mother is middle-aged; her hair has grey streaks in it, and her hairdresser is always asking her if she wants a rinse. She has a fat, round face with a funny but not big nose. Some people would say I inherited it. Her eyes are brown and her eyebrows are arched. She is about five feet four inches tall, and is always going to start slimming next week.

My mother has sides to her character. When my brother and I are good, she will joke and play with us when she has time. She stays calm when my brother or I have an accident. For instance, when I had my accident with a car, she arrived at the hospital very calm and smiling. As she has six brothers, she knows what boys are like. She lets me cover my wall with posters and pictures, and has given up the idea of wallpaper. I am allowed to keep my room almost as I like, but there are limits. When a 'James Bond 007' poster appeared on my wall she nearly drew the line, but now she just insists it's out of sight from the door.

Whenever I have a fight with my brother, and as usual he comes off worst, she gives us a lecture, and points to the mortal wound which I have inflicted upon him. She is always telling us how our life is centred around television, and we are idiots to watch some of the rubbish that is put on. When she is doing the washing-up and we are watching a good programme on television, she comes in and pretends to be an early Christian Martyr who never has any fun but is always working hard.

She is a member of the local Operatic Society, and goes around the house singing little ditties. She does 'supply' teaching at an Infants School, and is sometimes called out in the middle of the day. She likes gardening, and has made the garden look beautiful.

2.   From *Petticoat Lane*

All the furious energy was still there. It was commerce turned into pandemonium. A dionysiac frenzy possessed nearly everybody who had anything to sell. There were rows and rows of men selling overcoats, and no sooner had I set my eyes on the first of them than I thanked Heaven I was wearing an overcoat. If I had not been, they would have pounced upon me at once and hustled me into one of their 'smart raglan overcoats I tell you people at Eighteen Shillings, I tell you Eighteen, all right then, Seventeen Shillings, for the last time this overcoat at *Sixteen Shillings*'. A youth in front of me was jammed into one and compelled to buy it, and later I saw him wandering about in it, still with a dazed expression on his face. One little man, all nose and bowler hat, was savagely cutting trousers to pieces with a carving knife. I do not know why he did it, but nobody seemed surprised. Men selling large pink vases would hit them with a hammer. A fellow with razor strops to sell looked like a homicidal maniac. The sweat was streaming down his face, and one hand was bandaged and bloody. 'I'll now first take the edge off this razor', he bellowed, and then, in a fury, he picked up the razor, and attacked a block of wood with it. Later, when I passed, he was yelling, 'As the basis of this strop, people, you've got Carbonorum, the hardest substance known. Cuts glass, glass!' And the next moment there were showers of cut glass falling around him, through which you saw his eyes gleaming wildly.

3. From *Oliver Twist*
It was market-morning. The ground was covered, nearly ankle-deep, with filth and mire; and a thick stream, perpetually rising from the reeking bodies of the cattle, and mingling with the fog, which seemed to rest upon the chimney-pots, hung heavily above. All the pens in the centre of the large area, and as many temporary ones as could be crowded into the vacant space, were filled with sheep; tied up to posts by the gutter side were long lines of beasts and oxen, three or four deep. Countrymen, butchers, drovers, hawkers, boys, thieves, idlers, and vagabonds of every low grade, were mingled together in a dense mass: the whistling of drovers, the barking of dogs, the bellowing and plunging of oxen, the bleating of sheep, the grunting and squeaking of pigs; the cries of hawkers, the shouts, oaths, and quarrelling on all sides; the ringing of bells and roar of voices, that issued from every public-house; the crowding, pushing, driving, beating, whooping, and yelling; the hideous and discordant din that resounded from every corner of the market; and the unwashed, unshaven, squalid, and dirty figures constantly running to and fro, and bursting in and out of the throng—rendered it a stunning and bewildering scene, which quite confounded the senses.